Teaching the Designing

of

Decal and Handpainted China

Lustre Colors, and Effects
Gold Work, Lost Arts

by
George Ellwood Kulp

Edited & Published by Blessing Simmons

FIRST EDITION NOVEMBER, 1970

Printed in the United States of America
By
Atlantic Printers & Lithographers, Inc.
Miami, Florida

GEORGE ELLWOOD KULP

PREFACE

This book has been compiled to teach the art of decal arranging and hand painting on china, ceramic or glass. To present the idea of blending in decals with china paintings, so one cannot tell where the decals end and handpainting begins or how to use the decals as a pattern to paint by. The results:—a picture on china, ceramic or glass. Also the lustre effects over same.

After seventy years of experience, I wish to give to my students and future generation, my designs, color studies and a practical method of producing good work and to avoid any of the unpleasant surprises that can come in the decorating and firing of your china.

It is necessary, however, to give the directions from the beginning, for the benefit of the beginner, so this book may be used as a text book in schools, institutions and public libraries.

I, sincerely, hope to have succeeded in producing a text book to meet all the requirements for the painters of china and that our illustrations may help someone to enjoy many pleasant hours of the fine art of decal china painting and decorating.

Included, also, are a few lost arts, such as beaded lamp shades, candle decoration, satin or chamois painting.

GEORGE ELLWOOD KULP

INTRODUCTION

I have indexed this book for your convenience. However, after reading your book through carefully, it is well to re-read from time to time. This will be very helpful to students. If you are learning to china paint without a teacher, it is difficult but not impossible. You must be patient, read and study your textbook, and do your best.

Decorating a piece of china improves the appearance of the china, tells a story, decorates a corner or just a conversation vase. An attractiveness of food served up in dishes decorated with new and lovely designs and colors adds to a beautiful table. Decoration of china should stand for beauty in line, form and color. Daintiness is also returning again. You should choose your decoration to suit your china. Consider first the china you wish to decorate, then choose a decoration which is appropriate. If a vase or pitcher — Does your vase suggest grecian, roman, french, dutch, colonial or modern. Then your decorations should comply with the style and shape. If modern you can use a more liberal design. Always compose a design to the shape of vase or plate. Try to visualize and plan the picture on the vase or plate and then work your plan. Do not make useless scrolls and never too much decoration. It is not how much you can get on a vase or plate but how you plan them through simple lines and good proportions.

You will enjoy the various decals and decorations and be able to combine them to please yourself. Remember that good decoration is harmony and a well balanced article. Beautiful vases meant as a conversational vase will be seen from many points of view and should be so decorated that the vase, no matter from where it is seen will convey its meaning. Remember that the lower part of a vase should appear more solid than the top.

Never be afraid to cut out part of a decal that you wish to add to another to get the effect you want. A group of flowers made into a spray, on one side of a plate, as if they are growing, is good. Decals are made to be cut as needed as well as the way they are received by you. Sometimes they are fine but other times you may need a small bird in the skies or a small house in the distance.

The lost art of design outlining under lustre, will give you many rewards for your efforts. Try some of the beaded lampshades they are beautiful. We look forward to working with you with happy anticipation and with satisfaction that I have done my part in bringing about a new spirit to revive china decorating. For generations and generations, decal work was confined to a private room in china factories but now we all may have the pleasure of the work.

GEORGE ELLWOOD KULP

TABLE OF CONTENTS

CHAPTER ONE

You will notice that throughout this book we will stress cleanliness. One should not work on a cluttered table top. Have your working area organized and as dust free as possible. Dust is the enemy of china work. We stress patience.

Remember unity of design when composing. The different parts of decals to be used must have something in common and remember they share the same china. Do not bring together any contrasting ideas like colonial or roman with chinese birds or dragons or love birds, or a symmetrical landscape with flowers. If you are planning on a set of china dishes remember that decorations are to embellish the china, or if the china is to occupy a corner or use as a wall decoration, then let it tell a story or be more decorative. One must avoid too much decoration in the center of plates for china table ware. This book is composed primarily to design china for display use. Select china, plan design in keeping with the period of subject. Avoid over crowding. Make it well balanced. Keep your design and picture simple and always remember to connect different designs so that they will not appear to be isolated or suspended in mid air. If your movement is round and plate is round, let your lines of decoration, express a forward movement. This is obtained by the intersection of lines slightly bent towards a special direction, either connected or disconnected, one to succeed another.

You must also learn to first divide and subdivide your china. To plan your color scheme. Learn how to take care of your working equipment. Little by little you should make yourself a group of patterns, like different size circles, triangles, ovals, cup and plate dividers out of heavy cardboards or clear plastics. If you make a pattern, save it. Have a pattern file.

EQUIPMENT NEEDED

Large flat dish of water
Decal squeegee or long fibered cotton
Sharp scissors
Sm. bottle of adhesive for decals
Sm. bottle—oil of cloves
Sm. bottle lavender oil
Sm. bottle turpentine for oil
Old fashioned pen point and handle
Kulp's Roman Gold
Lazy susan marked with your plate divided as a banding wheel
Glaze paints
Flat ⅜" or ½" thin brush for adhesive
Flat ⅜" or ½" thin brush for ground oil
No. 3, 5, 8 square shader brushes
Pointed shader brush No. 2
Sable long hair liner brush
100 mesh or finer, white silica sand
Clean rags
China marking pencil (pointed)
Palette knife (flexible)

4"x4" (sandblasted fine or acid etched) plate glass on which to grind paints
China plate dividers
Several old cotton pieces (smooth)
Sm. dish for turpentine
Small wads or balls of cotton for dabber
Knife (stiff) square sharp end
Sm. bottle of medium
Sm. bottle of alcohol
Sm. bottle of gold Facilatator
Covered palette
Compass plate marker
2 pcs. old silk
Lambs wool, small wad
Modeling clay
Sm. bottle of grounding oil
Sm. bottle of tinting oil
Regular china paints
Red sable liner 0
No. 10 flat camel hair brush
Carbon paper and tracing paper
2 or 3 pcs. old T-shirt or equal
Patterns

NOTES

Colors to have on hand—Yellow green, yellow, yellow brown, azure blue glaze, olive green, capucine brown, french yellow red, to bring up faded poinsietta red, ivory, albert yellow, apple green, brown green, dark green, shading green, rose, blood red, ruby, russian green, banding blue, violet of gold, indigo blue, dark brown, orange, orange yellow, chrome green, deep blue, capucine red, black green, purple, elargo rose,

FIRING OF CHINA

Fire china at .016

Why fire china at .016 instead of .018? Because by firing china at .016 you bring out the colors in the decal more brilliant and the gold will be longer wearing.

.017 and .018 is not good for pinks as they will come out more a brown cast. Yellows will not be pure colors. By putting in decals and your gold work together at .016 they will fire where they don't always fire at .018.

Ceramic are to be fired .018 or .019 and glass at 022.

All manufacturers furnish instructions with their kilns and are willing to help you in time of need. You should also keep the kiln clean and free from dust.

Two pieces of china will stick together, if they are glazed. Never put heavy articles inside bowls or concave pieces, and if you run out of silts you can use asbestos shingle board pieces. They can be used under china and walls. Cracking of china is caused by uneven expansion of china. The bottom being heavier than the top and the thinner part expanding quicker than the bottom part and when the heat is strong, the cracking follows. A vase whose base is heavier on the bottom, should have a piece of asbestos paper under the base on a brick to insure even heat. Always leave a space between china pieces as when they expand with the heat they should not touch.

Sudden cold air draft can crack or craze china, so let it cool naturally. Never try to hurry it. Keep your plates stacked straight and steady. They may also be fired standing on edge or on top of certain pieces, except soft ware china.

Grays, blues and pinks stand the strongest firing, then comes green, yellow and browns. Next purple and last reds and flesh tones. Gold will always stand .016 on china. Keep you r soft ware china in the cooler part of the kiln.

Try to avoid decorating china that has been used as sometimes the glaze is affected by greasy substances already absorbed. Sometimes the results are not satisfactory.

Also sometimes after firing a decal on the china, it appears a little rough to the fingers. Simply sand with # 280 sanding paper. This is a very fine paper and cannot hurt decals or hand painted work, rubbed lightly.

Too strong a firing will sink the decorations and fire your color away, it will also give you a bubbled appearance, and the gold will be uneven and wavy.

A craze appearance is the result of over firing. I am trying to help you to know the results of our early errors. I sometimes even fire my hard glaze china at .013 and .014 but if I am doing some of the soft ware china I would still fire it at .016. Your decal colors turn out prettier.

DABBER OR PADS FOR BACK GROUNDS

Use old unpressed silk pieces. Preferably from an old scarf. Some may wish to use a wad of lambs wool with the silk tightly stretched over the wool and twisted, you may lightly dab in the background you have painted on with brush, being careful not to mix your colors together but to blend the edges together.

I prefer to make a dabber as follows: Take about 5" square piece of an old silk handkerchief, silk scarf or any other part of a worn silk dress. Put a wad of cotton or lambs wool in the center of the square and stretch the material smoothly over the cotton or wool to make a firm 1" or 1¼" ball. Tie. Cut excess string. Singe to remove lint. Now dab hard on a surface (not your work) to form a mashed ball. You are now ready for work.

Your silk dabber is used to make an even ground of color or the blending of one color with another color. Do not have any wrinkles in your mashed ball or it will show on the plate. Learn to pad quickly and remove your pad without pressing your dabber too hard on the colors. Always working in a light hammering way. With a little practice you will be able to dab and blend colors rather than remove color. Always go from light to dark in china work.

Now—to pad a sky for instance. Have your azure blue powder mixed and ready, this paint is thinned like a real heavy cream. Dip (or wet) your pad in a little medium, then pad lightly in paint, then lightly touch your sky. Remember light to dark. You can always apply more paint. Leave a small white area if you wish a cloud. Dab and blend around a cloud to make it look like one, It can be done. Takes a little patience and practice. If you are not satisfied, take your color off with turpentine and start over. After you have pleased yourself, let it set a short time and pick the plate up again and pad a little more where needed.

NOTES

Now if you wish to have different colors on a background of fruit or flowers, the process is the same, only pad each color separately and blend end the edges. Clean your edges if you wish to apply a band of gold.

We find that by starting with the pad instead of the brush that our padding time is less. We can apply more color where needed. The paint has a look of lightness. The background should be applied on your last fire. A good cotton is advisable (surgical has less bumps.)

To powder with a glaze or color on a background. First dry your plate in a warm oven. When cool use dusting wool and dust over the painting the dry powder color that is to be used. It is not necessary to use much pressure on the wool. If you are powdering, just a portion of some painting, it is best to place your dry powder about in the center of the place to be powdered, then rub it around gently spreading it carefully and near the edges of the designs. Do not allow much color thus causing the edges to blend in. Finally dust off all color that does not adhere to the painting. It is then ready to be fired.

Yellow brown is pretty, it is a light brown with a yellow tint. It is used in backgrounds, also for shading yellows and for blending greens. It will blend with light blue, light green, orange, reds and browns. May be shaded into chestnut brown or capucine brown and then will get a graduated brown background.

NOTES

CHAPTER TWO

DECALS

Decals are designs of different scenes, flowers, fruit, or figures painted on paper with china colors by a special process, developed many years ago. They are transferred to the china or ceramic to be fired and the paint of the decal is fired into the china.

WATERMOUNT DECALS

To begin, your plate must be perfectly clean. The watermount decals you always apply face up. First immerse the decal in luke warm water, twenty to thirty seconds. Lay it on a newspaper face up or shake the water from it gently and apply (face up) to china. Hold decal gently in place, if decal feels loose from the paper, pull the paper (easy does it) from under the decal. Remember face up. Make sure the decal is where you want it. Now gently pad water from under the decal, working from the center to edge of decal. Leave no wrinkles, bubbles or water, make sure it is smooth.

A decal squeegee is wonderful as it will squeeze all the water nicely from under the decal. Slightly tilt your plate and move it around under the light and you will easily notice if you h a v e all the air pockets from under the decal. (If you do not remove the water from under the decal, when it is fired, it will steam and burst in that one spot. Then the patch is hard sometimes to paint out.) Let your plate now dry. If you do not have a squeegee, use a piece of cotton (quilting cotton). It is stringy and you can wring it out when it gets water in it. Do not rub your decal, as it is tender,

but start from the center and slide gently to the edge and remove all bubbles.

STRIP TISSUE DECALS

Take your finger and rough an edge of the decal, then with your fingernail or a knife separate the backing paper and tissue. Strip the tissue containing the decal from the paper. Now you may follow the complete instructions of watermount decals. The difference —a thin tissue to remove from decal instead of heavy backing paper. Keep this pattern face up on the plate.

ADHESIVE DECALS

The plate or china must be very clean. Brushes must be clean. Use No. 10 flat brush for the adhesive and keep this brush for edhesive only. Now to begin, cut your decals to fit your plate. Arrange them on the plate to see if they fit and see if they are arranged the way you are planning the plate. Remember you are going to be applying this decal, FACE DOWN. Now that you have measured and marked your plate and have your ideas in your mind, put the adhesive on the plate. In applying the adhesive don't pick up too much on your brush and strip your brush on both sides before you start applying the adhesive to the plate. Remember you are putting on adhesive, just enough to glue your decal to the plate. It must be smoothly and thinly applied. Do not skip a spot. Slant your plate, it will tell you if you have put your adhesive on smoothly. Set aside for about

17

NOTES

twenty minutes, by this time it will become tacky. Test it, if it is sticky then you are ready to put on your decal.

Strip the paper from back of trimmed decal by taking your finger and roughing an edge of decal, then with fingernail or sharp knife separate the backing from the decal. Now apply your decal face down. Smooth out and press down gently and firmly, hold a second with your finger, leave as few wrinkles as possible. It will stick and take hold of the china. All air must be out from under it. If a tiny wrinkle appears, press down and stretch lightly. (You can also take Dad's old shaving brush—gather the bristles together with a rubber band and kind of trim your bristles flat). This makes a stiff brush to adhere the design to an adhesive plate before applying the water to remove the tissue. You hammer gently the decal before removal of the paper, it will help to hold the decal and make it stick to china better. Pouncing it not from the elbow movement but from a wrist action. (Now you have renamed Dad's shaving brush to a pouncing brush). Remember, you are gluing the decal to the china. Now you are ready to remove the paper from the decal. (I use the quilting cotton or upholstery cotton because it is stringy. You can wring out the cotton when it has absorbed water and straighten it out flat and use again). Wet your cotton and press the decal down firmly with the wet cotton all over. Let it set a second, add a little water. As the tissue frees itself from the decal, it begins to wrinkle. Test it. If it comes off free, take a sharp little tool, lift the edge carefully and remove the wet paper from the decal. If it sticks a little, press down gently, it will usually release itself. If it does not release from the paper in that little spot, you will need to paint this spot, but this can be eliminated by patience. Now you have the paper from the decal. Sometimes I submerge the cup in water to thoroughly wet the paper from the decal. It will slide off easy, if wet enough.

Next, wring your cotton out dry, as possible, and press down gently all over to dry your wet decal. Remember it is tender, so do not press hard. Wring your cotton pad often and be sure your pad is straightened out flat again after wringing. One can also use a small sponge or chamois. When you have removed the water, let your plate dry for a day and fire china .016. If you have only a scene in the center of the plate, and you plan on drawing a circle of gold around the scene, it is advisable to fire this scene first before applyng your gold as the gold will fire away if applied to adhesive. Also if you have all your decal design in and you wish to fire only one time and you wish to apply a band of gold, remove the adhesive from the rim of plate with turpentine. If you fail you can always take the adhesive off with turpentine and the decal also before firing. So have courage, it is fun.

Some people use a chamois to dry and it works satis-

factorily but I do not. In the factory of yesteryear, the decorated ware, after the decal is applied to adhesive, is placed in water only long enough to dissolve the tissue and it will slide off easily. Any part of the decal which does not adhere firmly should be patted in place with a moist cotton, and then it is dried for firing. Now I know this is quite lengthy but once you do it and learn correctly, you will really enjoy applying them, once you have achieved success. Sometimes I let my decals dry two days.

CONVERTED ADHESIVE DECALS TO WATERMOUNT DECALS

Some people would rather work with watermount decals only, so for the adhesive decals there is a special mixture you can purchase. (You can spray or brush this mixture on the decal). If you spray, crisscross a few times, as the spray will apply the solution too ligthly. This solution should be heavier. Let it dry four to five hours or overnight. Yau apply this material to the face side of the decal, as you will be removing the paper, after the solution has dried. Be sure your decal decoration or sheet of decal is free of dirt, or you can use a ½" brush to apply this material. Next, after the decal has dried, separate the tissue and decal from the backing paper. Immerse decal in clean water for a few seconds, apply decal to china face up. Remove tissue film of the special mixture you have applied and dry out air bubbles and excess water by working from center outwards. You must be very careful as this decal will tear easily. Dry overnight before firing. Fire china 016.

After firing decals they may be painted or padded and even dusted in the same manner as regular hand painted china is done. It is a touchy matter to apply china paints before the first fire to the decals and you should really be more experienced before you try to do this, for they must be perfectly dry and you must be very careful. So wait for your second fire for touchup.

Blistering or air bubbles are a very common fault with decals and this is caused by not removing all the air bubbles under the decal and not drying the decals, hence steam in the kiln under the spot. So remember to dry your decals with squeegee or cotton.

Adhesive decals you can not separate, are old ones. You apply them the same way as adhesive decals, except you will be wetting the heavy paper, then they will slide off, face down. There are not too many of these around at this time. So remember if you cannot separate your adhesive decal, trim, apply adhesive and apply decal with backing, face down. Wet, remove and dry.

NOTES

DECAL DESIGNING

When you have selected the decals you are going to use, you may want to cut them to fit your pattern or plate. Rearrange it on the plate or vase to see if you like it. The trouble with students today, they buy a decal and stick it in the middle of the plate and put some gold around the edge and they think it is beautiful, and it is, but by thinking a little, you can arrange other decals in many different and beautiful ways. The same as painting a picture. No artist goes and puts a cow in the middle of a plate. The artist puts maybe a barn in the distance and a little grass around and blends in a sky with a bird, maybe a tree or a creek. Well, this is what I wish to teach you to do in this book.

First select your china plate, vase, pitcher or what you wish, design a scene with decals, maybe a dancing girl under an arbor of flowers or grapes. You will be able to find the decals for same. They will need to be small and the arbor can be drawn.

You may wish to make a spray of flowers on a plate, Decals can be cut and applied. Make it look like a flower or vine growing up the side of the plate. Keep in mind while you are decorating a flower or vine and how it looks in real life. Don't be afraid to cut up decals to make yourself a beautiful spray of flowers. You will be amazed at the designs you can make. Sometimes one has two large sprays, one above the other, and you need a top so make it a little smaller spray and join them together by trimming before removing the decals from the paper backing. Fill in extra blooms or buds. Remember to trim your decals so they connect but do not overlap.

A beautiful plate might comprise two-inch roses around the edge. Then you may put a design of Kulp's roman gold around the edge or a band of Kulp's roman gold. When you use the ransom styled plate with rose or fruit around the plate, the band of gold is applied to all the edge including the waves of the china around the edge, except the small indentations. These are pretty when you have applied a little color of light green, rose or blue in them, which ever color harmonizes with your decals. On a large plate you may want to apply a scalloped band of gold. This is applied with your pattern and china pencil, then you apply your gold. We suggest Kulp's formula of roman gold No. 1, it will outwear liquid gold. No. 2, Kulp's gold, reminds one of the gold color as it appears down through the ages. I think plain liquid gold is gaudy in appearance.

On the violet plate (shown on the multiple picture) a circle of color is put in and connected to the violets to give your plate balance. This band is easily applied with china colors and a pen point.

I use glaze for retouching because the glaze finishes with a finer finish and will blend better with what you are up against. Glazes are ground finer than regular paints so you therefore get a better, smoother coat on the last coat.

A fruit plate is beautiful. Use about four of the five inch decals of fruit (different fruits). Place them on a 10" plate. Put a cherry or small nut, maybe three, between the patterns. Put a gold band around the plate edge. This can all be done in one fire. Dry and fire .016.

Remember, take your time, put your thoughts to what you are doing. (Art work will help you forget about the worries of the world). So relax, you can do it. If you fail the first time you can always remove it.

CENTERING DECAL DESIGNS

Wash and dry plate well. Leave no lint on it. Cleanliness is essential.

Take a round dish or saucer the size of whatever decal you are using. Place decal back on it, mark and cut decal the size of dish. Use the same saucer or dish to mark your plate. Be sure the circle is in the middle of the dish and you have used your divider and gauge. Now mark in a circle in the dish with a china marking pencil. Now you are ready to proceed with your application of decal. You can test your center by taking your gauge and marking your circle. Set your gauge so it is the same size.

OUTLINE WORK

You can use liquid gold, roman gold or Kulp's roman gold for outline for your emblem or name on the back of china.

Remember to sign your china, either by name or emblem. Design yourself an emblem to put on the back of your china.

Use black, brown, green or any other dark colors you like. Grind your powder well and mix with a little medium and thin it with oil of cloves. It will fire black or the color you choose. Use your pen point. This will save your gold.

Now should you wish an outline to paint by, mix the color of your choice, black, brown, green with a little water and add two drops of mucilage or sugar syrup. Only water will remove this outline. If it dries on your palette add a little water.

India ink and china marking pencils will fire away on china the first fire. But India ink may be painted over and not smear into your color.

NOTES

In the back of this book, we have several designs, should you desire, you may use for china painting.

DECAL REMOVER OR CHINA ERASER

To erase fired colors, or fired gold, use what is called china eraser, which is a composition made up of muriatic acid and hydrofluoric acid.

FORMULA—one-half hydrofluoric acid
one-half rust remover

These can be purchased at the local drug stores, if your china supply store does not have china remover. Hydrofluoric will attack glass, so use a Polyethylene bottle, no metal or glass. You can also use pure muriatic acid, it is not quite so dangerous and is a little slower. It is not wise to use hydrofluoric acid alone as it will eat through the china, glaze or enamel. One should wear rubber gloves when using the acid. *Acid is dangerous.* REMEMBER you cannot tell by looking if acid is on your hands or under your nails. Watch that you do not spill it. Watch how you lay the cap down and where you lay it. What end of the swab you have put in the acid and where you have laid the swab that has been dipped in acid. WATER will wash it completely off but it will still burn for 3 or 4 hours and if it gets under your nail you will have severe discomfort and pain. So handle it directly from a small wide mouth bottle, 1" or 1½" diameter and be sure it is placed in a container that you cannot knock over easily. Use a stick or cotton swab, apply it to the parts to be removed, taking care not to go over any other part of the color. Let it set a second and rub with the cotton swab. Rinse with water and apply it twice if necessary, or until the color is removed. Rinse and dry. Remove and dry. The China may be repainted or you may apply more decals.

Remember — Remember — handle the stick from the same end. You cannot be too careful. When acid eats your skin it is treated the same as a burn.

Discard your rags and swabs you have been using, in acid so you will not forget and use them again. Acid inflicts a painful burn.

MIXING CHINA PAINTS AND GLAZES

Mix a few drops of medium oil with your regular powder colors. Have the desired quantity of powder color on the ground glass or slab or palette. Stir and grind well in a circular motion until the color has become mixed together and is smooth and a little stiff.

You do not want it in a runny condition, but should be a working consistency. Too much oil will cause the colors to shrink and run and destroys your color, making them too pale and they have a washed out appearance after firing. Blistering of colors is sometimes caused by bad oil and will have the same bad effect on heavy or medium heavy tints.

Try to put out only the amount of powder you need but should you have a little left over then be sure they are kept free of dust and lint until you use them again. You will remix them when ready to use again, as they will dry out. One needs to be especially careful with dark colors that they are not too thin.

If you wish your glazes to work a little better, then mix it very thoroughly. Glazes are mixed the same as china paints. I cannot tell you how important it is to grind and mix your colors. Grind it and grind again. Your glaze should also be a heavy consistency, then thin it with a little tinting oil to a consistency where it will run off your knife. It is then ready to work. You use a flat brush and pull your strokes one way. When you are using the dabber, wet your pad a little with tinting oil before you dip into your glaze.

REMEMBER, when mixing paint, mix first with medium, then tinting oil. China colors and glaze paint fires into china, while enamel paint stays on top of china.

Enamel colors are mixed with enamel medium, and must be stringy to be applied.

DO's AND DON'T's

Do clean your brushes and tools with clear turpentine, and in laying them away, see that they have a straight natural shape. Try to develop the habit of pressing a brush on a piece of blotting paper or cloth that is not full of lint. See that your brush is not cramped and it is allowed to dry straight.

- o -

Do use a few drops of tinting oil in the mixing of colors. It will keep your paint open to work with them. But do not use only more than a few drops, as too much will cause the colors to run, especially in hot weather, so be careful. Turpentine encourages the colors to dry quickly.

- o -

Do paste your design to your carbon paper with a little tape, when copying then it does not slip.

- o -

Do buy good brushes and materials. Keep them free from lint and dust.

- o -

NOTES

Use small cotton wrapped around point of toothpick to clean up work on outline or point of wax china pencil to pick up lint, or bristles from your brush or dirt on plate. Or an orange stick with a dull point.

- o -

If you like, after cleaning brushes with turpentine, give them a touch of olive oil to keep them soflt, but this is not necessary.

MISTAKES WE CAN MAKE

Paint should not be applied too thickly, it will chip off.

Always grind your powder on an acid etched or sandblasted glass.

Do not fire greenware ceramic at the same time, in the same kiln, with china which has decals applied for firing. The dust from the greenware will be picked up on your decals on the china, leaving a rough, dusty appearance. And besides the greenware is fired at a different cone than .016.

Kiln must be free of dust when firing china or glass.

Color not ground enough or too much oil used.

Be sure your brushes are clean.

Badly ground color will look rough and gritty.

Mixing more paint than we need.

Remember to turn gold over while working with it, every time you stick your brush in it almost. It will settle quickly.

Do soak a new brush in turpentine, alcohol or water, this will take out the loose hairs.

Overfiring will destroy your work. Fire as told. Firing too much can fire away decoration.

NOTES

CHAPTER THREE

GOLD WORK

Always buy good brushes and good gold. You will need a pen point and holder to apply the gold filigree. A short red sable for paste or gold. No. 1, 2 or 3 brush. A No. 00,0, or, red sable liner is good for outlining. A deerfoot brush No. 7 or 8.

Keep your brushes and spatula knife especially for gold. Cleaning them with gold facilitator or oil of lavender.

Liquid gold comes in liquid form and it is best to have a small tile to put several drops on and brush from it or use your finger in a circular movement to pick up your gold. Try to be neat and keep it in a half-inch or smaller spot. Gold may be applied to the edge of plates, cup edges or tops of vases with the ball tip of your finger, by rubbing gold evenly all around. I have always found if I wish to use my gold brush it is good to first have seven or eight drops on my tile, let it set five minutes and pick it up with my brush or finger, therefore I do not get enough on the brush to run from the design I wish to place the gold on. Be sure it is applied evenly and not too thin and not too thick either. Let it dry before firing and fire at .016 on china. Liquid gold does not need to be polished after firing. If your gold is applied too thick, it will peel or flake off and if applied too thin, it will look purple. Fired gold may be removed with liquid china eraser. Unfired gold with facilitator, lavender oil or turpentine.

Always fire in decals first before applying gold as gold over fresh decals will fire away.

Try to work in dust free conditions and never thin your gold with turpentine. Always use gold facilitator, if you do thin your gold. Remember to stir it often while using as the gold will settle and the thinner comes to the top. Try to make a good line in one, single long stroke. By going over the lines, an uneven appearance sometimes appears. Never apply liquid gold near wet colors as it will run into the colors.

GOLD DUSTING

Gold dusting is done by applying the powdered roman gold or unfluxed gold over a coat of liquid bright gold. This will dry quickly and should therefore be applied quickly, so it will be wet enough for the powder to adhere to. The effect—a dull finish which makes a ground for your etchings.

RAISED PASTE GOLD WORK

First sketch your design on the china. Now take your raised paste powder, grind it good with your medium for raised paste and use only enough of the medium to hold the powder together, like a thick paste. Now thin, stirring it again, and every so often breathing upon it until it will string from your knife. It will need to hang onto your brush and you will need to pick up your paste from under the center of your pile, so that the paste will transfer from your brush to an even line on your china. Try to make it in a single long stroke. Now remember the line should be high and round like a little

27

NOTES

cord or string. If it flattens, your mixture is too oily, so breathe upon it to put a little moisture in it and stiffen it up.

Your dot paste must be stiffer than your paste for lines. If you make a mistake, try to clean it with your wooden pick or a brush slightly moistened with turpentine. Your brush may be cleaned in turpentine when it is clogged with paste but do not thin your paste with turpentine. Let it air dry. Your work should look dull when it is ready for firing. If it is shiny, it is too oily or not dry and may spread or run during the firing. Paste may be applied over fired colors or lustres as well as on white china. It must be well dried without artificial means before firing. Gold should be applied after paste is fired. Fire .016.

KULP'S ROMAN GOLD LOOKS BETTER - WEARS LONGER

Recipe: To one plaque of Roman gold, drop ten drops of liquid bright gold. Thoroughly mix it and breathe on the gold as you mix it. Gold must be entirely loose from slab and thin down with five drops of gold facilitator and it is ready to be put in a small jar. Don't forget to thoroughly mix. When it is ready, it should drop from your brush in a loose clean drop, not a sluggish drop. Only then is it ready to apply. If you let it set a day after you have mixed it, the gold facilitator sometimes evaporates so you must add a drop or so. Liquid gold gives the roman gold more body.

- o -

Always apply Kulp's Roman gold in one direction. Stir every other time you dip your brush in the gold as the gold will settle. After the gold is applied, let it stand until dry. Sometimes it dries sooner than other times. Whenever you fire, fire .016 on china, glass .022, ceramic .018 or .019. Kulp's Roman gold when fired has the appearance of light gold matt. Rubbing or burnishing is required to bring out its natural brilliancy (see burnishing chapter).

If you are ready to apply an edge and you do not wish to use your banding wheel, you may put some of Kulp's Roman gold on your tile and with the ball tip of your finger (in a circular motion) pick up some gold and apply the gold to the edge of plates, edge of cups or vases. Making sure you apply it evenly and go around it two or three times to be sure you have not missed any spots.

When drawing designs or following the designs of the white china, try to make your line with a single long stroke instead of many short strokes, as the short strokes makes an uneven appearance. Hold your fingers on your brush down close to your work.

DO NOT HANDLE YOUR UNBURNISHED GOLD as dust and perspiration from your fingers will show badly. I always burnish the gold after each firing. Roman gold after firing is unburnished or dead gold. You burnish this gold to get a high light and to bring life to the gold. Roman gold may also be used without mixing as recommended by applying a few drops of facilitator and burnish as instructed.

BURNISHING OF GOLD

I burnish our gold with water and #100 or #180 mesh silica sand or finer. Simply by taking a piece of soft cloth (old cotton T shirt is ideal), dip it in the water and then dip it in the sand and rub the gold lightly and evenly until its proper color is obtained. Use plenty of water. Burnish gold every time before handling china or reapplying gold. As we stated before, unburnished gold will absorb fingerprints. When you have polished your gold so it looks good, set your plate aside. The sand will dry and you can wipe sand away easily or if you are in a hurry, wash the china with water.

Some people like to use agate for burnishing. It will give a pleasing appearance to your gold but is a little slow. We do not recommend the glass burnishers, as sometimes they leave little glass fibers and these leave bad marks, and sometimes get in your paint. You must be very careful when using the glass burnishers. They do a nice job but leave their fine particles to worry about later.

If when burnishing, your gold rubs off, you have underfired your china and must apply some more and fire again. When gold is applied too thick it will peel or flake off. If overfired, gold will look pale.

Should your gold turn a deep brown after firing, apply Kulp's roman gold over this gold as a liquid gold will not fire on it and cover your work.

Always remember to use facilitator for thinning your gold, oil of lavender or gold facilitator. Never use turpentine for thinning. Liquid gold will soften Roman gold quickly. Kulp's Roman gold fired, may be removed with china eraser. If your gold plaque is cold, place it on a hot water bottle or equal. By warming it a little it will mix better.

Straight Roman gold mixed with liquid bright silver will give the effect of platinum. Gold may also be applied over fired silver or silver over fired gold. White enamel may be applied over fired gold.

NOTES

GOLD BANDING

Banding will require practice and a steady hand. If you have a banding wheel, it is wonderful but if not, put your plate in the center of a lazy susan or a disk. Then take your divider and mark lines on this disk itself so you will be able to place many different articles on the disk. This way you will be able to center your plate. When you get it set inside the line you wish, stick on the back of the plate some children's modeling clay or wax or rope caulking. Three or four little balls will secure your plate. Then rest your arm on a higher support so as to keep the brush in a steady position, touch the china lightly and move the plate around. If you are drawing a circle, use a deerfoot brush. When applying gold, work gold and brush so you have plenty of gold in it and it is pointed. Hold steady and line up your banding wheel and now you take your time, turn the wheel, hold your brush steady and round we go, easy does it. To make a small band, use a thin brush, but a broader brush to make a larger band. Let your brush run over the same round line a few times until it looks good. If you have a little dab, take your orange stick or heavy paper pencil point and clean up the little dab.

REMEMBER DO NOT USE YOUR GOLD BRUSHES FOR COLORS. HAVE YOUR BRUSHES FOR GOLD ONLY.

Bands are made in gold, silver and color. They can be made with ground oil and dusting with powder as in the background work. This will give good results on a broad band and it will be even. Use a deerfoot brush for this groundlaying. Always make a line in one long stroke, do not try to dab in short strokes.

And of course you can always do your banding with your index finger. By holding your plate flat and using the fleshy part of the finger. Dip finger in your gold tile and then rub round the edge of plates.

GOLD LEAFING: NO FIRING

Gold leaf is very thin leaves purchased in a small book. It is very difficult to apply and you can break a leaf or the slightest puff of air will blow it from you.

(1) First clean the ornament thoroughly, cut out all unnecessary parts,, then give it two thin coats of shellac, when dry give it one coat of oil gold sizing and let dry overnight. Apply this size with a stiff brush and use sparingly.

(2) In the morning use a thin brush, about 3 inches wide. Hold your book of gold leaves in your left hand and with your right hand, lift cover and bend back about one quarter way, then with index finger nail run it across the leaf, which cuts the leaf, then take the gilding tip brush and brush it across your hair (the hair being a little oily), lift the leaf properly. Then press it lightly on exposed part of leaf, pull out a ¼" to break the leaf part, then lift it, put and press lightly on the gold size. When the ornament is gilded press a piece of cotton to the gold all over, then with a camel hair brush dust the loose gold off (which you save and resell). When finished rub a clean piece of cotton over gold to remove all roughness. (Not recommended for china. Use in decoupage work or gold leafing of furniture.

FILIGREE OR SERPENTINE WORK IN GOLD OR SILVER

Use Kulp's Roman gold.

On filigree work, use the old fashioned pen point and pen. Dip pen in gold and clean excess amount from point and proceed. Stir that gold every few minutes and clean your pen point, as gold can dry on edge and you do not wish any dots.

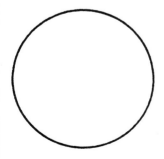

GOLD BAND

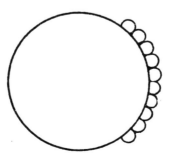

First row
on Gold Band

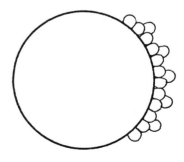

Second row
on Gold Band

NOTES

Apply a circle of gold around your decal. Sometimes it is better to put your filigree work inside to fill up the circle more but if there is not enough room to make it look good, then filigree your work on the outside of circle. Always fire in decals first before applying gold, as gold over fresh decals will fire away.

Now you have your circle made. Next start with small loops, attaching each to the gold band. Stir that gold. On the second row, attach every other one at the top with another loop. Stir that gold.

After your filigree work is completed, if you desire, put on your band around the edge. Dry and fire your china .016.

This does not necessarily have to be a center circle. It can be small oval circles. Even can be filigree around the edge of a plate. Wherever you think it would look good.

The more even your little loops are, the prettier your plate will be. But remember to stir your gold.

To do serpentine gold work on your plate or vase, the serpentine line will be a snake like line. First, you apply your loops to the inside of your lines, then draw a serpentine line all through the pattern. Now you fill

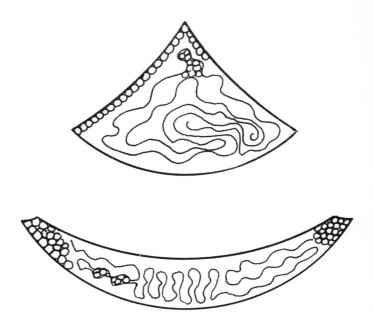

in all the other spaces with small circles. Keep your gold mixed.

Fill in completely with circles of gold. Fire china .016. Then burnish. Try to make your circles round and of equal size.

NOTES

CHAPTER FOUR

CHINA JEWELRY

China jewelry blanks are available. Use your small china medallion, place the small size decal (sized to fit medallion) or should it need to be trimmed, do so before applying decal to china. Place decal on china and mark around it and trim to size. Follow decal instructions and proceed the same as on a plate or vase.

If you desire a bouquet of flowers, cut small flowers out and put them on medallion, then draw a ribbon to tie them or put on a small vase or basket, it will look lovely. Old faces are especially beautiful on medallions. Now finger band the edge with Kulp's Roman gold. Fire .016 and after firing, burnish.

Sometimes on small jewelry, put designs or initials in with gold, dry and fire. On the second fire, if you desire, spray light green lustre over entire surface and fire again, or put in coral enamel in dots or small space with the light green lustre and fire. Beautiful.

Earrings, pins, cuff links, tie tacks, china knobs. All are beautiful when decorated.

HAND PAINTING

First, draw your design with India ink, with an ink pen or liner brush, on your china. If your design is a difficult one, it may be traced with the tracing paper and then transferred to china with carbon paper. Lay your tracing paper and your design and transfer by going over every line in the design. After you have finished this, take your carbon paper and your design on tracing paper and again trace every line in the design on to the china. Now remove tracing and carbon paper and draw your lines in with India ink. Do not make the lines too heavy. You may use a sharp stick or skewer to remove some of the ink. Your design on the china is now ready to paint.

In mixing your powder colors, mix with a few drops of medium (not too much, as your paints must be thick consistency and not too thin) grind well. It is very important to be sure all little bumps are ground well. Now when you are ready to paint: dip your brush in medium, pad it flat on a cloth and dip in paint. If paint seems too heavy, dip your brush in a little turpentine, pickup your paint with the side of the brush in a circular or half circular motion. Don't try to load your brush with all the paint you can get in it as you must remember in china painting, you paint light to heavy, and too much color applied on the first fire sometimes chips.

Now you are ready to tint in lightly your first coat of china paint. Maybe you have drawn a bouquet of chrysanthemums. So line in one chrysanthemum with rose color for the pink chrysanthemum, another one is yellow, so use jonquil yellow. Tint in leaves and stems, using deep chrome green and a little yellow brown. For small tops of leaves a little apple green and albert yellow. Now fire china .016. On the second painting, use rose on the pink and on the yellow, use a little bright yellow and a little orange and light brown for the shadows. REMEMBER TO MAKE SHARP STROKES here and there about the center so it will show petals. On the stems and leaves, use apple green, light green

NOTES

and light brown and a little rose. Remember to high-light and deepen your shadows. Fire. On the third painting, repeat same colors and fire again.

If you wish to make violet of iron, use a mix of ruby and brown. To make violet of gold, use a mix of ruby and blue. For deep purple, use ruby, dark blue and violet of gold. To make gray, use yellow, blue and rose. For a cold blue gray use more blue. Gray is not a good color to use first in painting of china.

If you have drawn a narcissus for your first paint-ing, use jonquil yellow for the centers and in the white leaves, use gray mixed with deep blue orange and rose. For stems and leaves, use apple green, light brown and a little deep chrome green. Fire .016. On the second painting use gray for shading the leaves and light brown for shading yellow centers'. For stems and leaves ,use brown, deep green and a little shading brown. Use brown for shadow leaves and a little ruby. Remember to highlight your leaves and flowers and give another coat of jonquil yellow to the flowers. Fire .016. On third painting, use same colors and deepen your shadow.

Some roses you use rose and ruby mixed. Make your leaves a dark green. For the stems and leaves, use orange and deep chrome green. Fire. Remem-ber to highlight your roses and leaves. If necessary, leave the china white in spots. Repeat on the second painting just a little deeper and use a little light brown in your leaves. Fire. On the third painting, repeat the same colors. This way you slowly apply your deep colors. Always remember to put your thorns in for the stems on roses. A pretty orange, yellow and rose color mixed, makes a beautiful rose. Shading where necessary with a little light brown and rose mixed. On a pink rose, use your rose color with apple green and light brown and shading green for the stems and leaves. Fire. On the second painting, shade your roses and remember to highlight and to shadow with a little deeper color.

Ruby is pretty for thorns with a little apple green at tip. For the yellow rose, use jonquil yellow and a brighter shade of yellow. Shade with darker color. For moss rose bud, use rose, for dark red rose, use deep purple and rose mixed. For a moss rose bud use your brush as a stipple to get the effect.

Tulips—paint in lightly with rose for the pink ones, ruby or deep purple for some bright stripes, capucine red and orange, some yellow for your leaves and stems, chrome green, shading green and yellow brown. Fire, but highlight. On the second painting, use rose, ruby or deep purple and striped with same colors but put in a few shadows by a mixture of banding blue and yellow, on your stems and leaves and a little orange at the bottom of tulips. Shade and highlight your flowers

and fire. Repaint your painting a third time with same colors, highlight and shadow and fire.

Purple pansies—use violet of gold and deep blue. In dark center, use deep blue alone. For yellow pansies, use albert yellow and jonquil yellow and orange with center of deep purple. On the second painting, shade your purple pansies with violet of gold and ruby. Yellow centers with orange yellow. Yellow pansies with gray or a mixture of blue and brown. Leaves and stems, chrome green, shading green and yellow.

At Christmas time—The holly berry, use capucine red. Leaves, chrome green and a little yellow mixed. Your stems capucine brown. Fire. On the second paint-ing, shade your berries with brown and highlight leaves and put your veins in the leaves.

On the Mistletoe—Use yellow, rose and blue for berries, stems and leaves chrome green and yellow and brown. Fire. On the second painting use the same colors to shade darker.

So it is summer and you wish to do Clover Blossom. Use rose for pink blossoms, apple green and orange yellow. Leaves, chrome green and apple green. Bring out your petal blossoms and veins of flowers and leaves.

A fruit plate, your colors for strawberries, capucine red and take a sharpened stick and remove some of the paint for the seeds, highlight by making one side lighter than the other. Dot the seeds with yellow. For Apricots use rose mixed with yellow and light brown or orange. Shade with a little blue and orange mixed. For cherries, violet of gold. For the dark cherries, fire first coat dark green and wash over it with a coat of crimson purple on the next fire. Highlight first. For red cherries, use yellow or poppy red for the light parts and dark red pompadous for the shadows.

Use dark pompadous for currants. Plums, use band-ing blue and crimson purple or deep blue and violet of gold.

When tinting your china, have your colors a little thinner with tinting oil so they will blend well. Use a broad flat camel hair brush and paint your china with several colors which are in your painting or a color that will blend well. Now let your plate dry a few minutes and prepare your pads for padding. Now pad and blend the colors and pad and blend until the excess paint is removed and you have a nice airy plate. Re-move the paint with a cloth (dipped in a little turpen-tine) before entirely dry, the width you want your gold lines or bands. When the tinting is very dry you may put your gold on. Tinting should only require one firing. To tell if your color is on smooth, tilt your plate a little so that the light will shine on it.

NOTES

A good color combination is turquoise, rose, apple green and salmon.

SHADOWS

The principle that decides the shading of a single flower or blossom applies equally well to two or more as well as the laws of light from some given direction. You must first decide the direction from where the light comes, from the upper left or right at an angle of 45 degrees and where the surface to be considered is concave or convex. The convex will always throw a shadow away from the sun. It is palest at the highest point. A concave surface is lighter around its edges and dark around its deepest parts. The center of a nasturtium from which the stamen springs being farthest from the light, is the deepest shadow. Around the edge of this where the petal bends back, it will be light. The stamens will cast shadows on the parts beneath. Do not forget the highlights.

The petals that first catch the light would naturally be the lightest. All parts of each petal will not receive the same portions of paint. Some will retire in the shadows while some parts curl upwards to the light. Your sheltered petals will be shadows when one petal is beneath the other.

A dark green ground is dusted with ruby or crimson purple before the second fire. It has a beautiful effect.

Leaves must always present a crisp appearance. The color being applied with as few strokes as possible. Leave all detail work for the second fire. And remember to try to make the leaf in one stroke. Put your shadows in first and fire and then on the second painting, put in the highlights. Then when painting on the third fire, touch up more depth in color and shadows. Don't forget to paint the way you wish your leaf to grow and put your veins in.

LEAVES

You cannot guarantee a law regarding leaves. If the sun is up the shadows are minor, if the sun is going down it will make a shadow, so it is according to how you make the flower and what time of day you wish the plate to tell in regards to your shadow. You will look at your plate and bring out the highlights and put in your shadows as this will alone make the plate beautiful. Yellow green mixed a little with olive green makes a good shadow. Sometimes olive green and black green, sometimes olive green with a little even shading where leaf is shadowed, brings out the design better.

If your leaves have vein in the middle then you paint

from each side of the dividing line. If you want to outline it, leave your flat brush do it but use the flat edge of the brush and by pulling your glaze from the edge to the center of the leaf. You will give a shadow to the leaf. By using the flat brush you can pull your stroke one way.

DRY DUSTING OR BACKGROUND WORK

First china must be very, very clean and your table or working area very clean. You will need tinting oil, grounding oil, powdered color desired, turpentine, square brush, deerfoot brush, cotton pad tied up in silk (one inch diameter), knife and cuticle stick of wood and a lint free rag. Now you are ready to begin work. We will do a plate.

Take a 10½" plate of china. Select a decal you like. Take a round dish or saucer the size of decal. Lay the dish on decal and mark around it. Be sure you have chosen a dish to fit the decal. Cut decal now to fit dish. Use your divider on the china or your gauge and use the same dish and draw a circle in the center of the plate, so the decal may be placed in circle. Now wipe china clean around the circle. Then you edge in ground oil with a pointed liner brush around the circle. See that no lumps or bubbles have appeared while stirring with your knife. Now apply quickly to the rest of surface outside of the circle to the edge of plate but leave enough not covered with grounding oil for your band of gold. Do not worry about the strokes. Only be careful to cover every little space, where you are applying the color. Let china set for one-half hour. Now while it is drying to become tacky, make a little ball pad (two of them). This pad is cotton tied up in silk. Pad should be an inch in diameter and very tightly tied. Have free from lint. Dip the pad in a little tinting oil and pad off excess so no shadows show. Pad off all excess ground oil. Be sure there are no shadows or light and heavy places, as these will show after firing. It should have the appearance of a lightly tinted surface. It would be well to also now use the second pad to make it smoother. Let it set for half hour or until tacky. It must be tacky to apply your powder. If your grounding oil is not tacky, the powder does not adhere properly to it.

Now be sure your powder color you are using is a powder, if necessary grind it on your slab or sieve it so there are no small particles or bumps. Now your surface is tacky, brush on powder (color desired) on plate. Hold plate horizontally, use deerfoot brush No. 10. Powder on generously but only lightly touch your plate. Do not let powder drop off plate but spread it all over the oil in kind of a circular motion over and

NOTES

over very lightly and be sure again you have covered it all and it shows no shadows for if you have shadows it means there is still oil in the grounding oil, so apply powder and it will absorb the powder. Now you may remove excess powder with your soft brush. This leaves a dull soft look (similar to a greased pan when floured for baking cakes). Never let your fingernail touch china (when dusting) accidentally. If you do not have a deer-foot brush, use a very, very soft brush, so it will not scratch surface. I use a deerfoot brush because it is slanted and soft.

Be sure your edges are cleaned up to where you want them. There should be no stray dust on the plate. You should be very thorough, cleaning your plate of excess powder. If it shows a crack or default it is better now to stop and take it all off and start over, as it will show when fired. Do not finger the dusted surface. Any excess powder left on plate will fire in also ,that is why you want to remove any excess powder from inside the circle or on the band edge of plate. If this is done rightly, your plate will come out with a solid beautiful color and then you can apply the gold decals after firing. Fire .016.

After the first fire, put in decal in circle and your gold flower decals around your decal in center and your gold band. Fire again .016. Now use a half circle cardboard or plastic pattern to mark in design around gold decal as picture shows, then you are ready to proceed with the gold serpentine effect. (See chapter on Serpentine). Serpentine the gold and join all lines in tiny circles. Put another gold band around edge and fire again, .016. Your plate should come out beautiful and a delight for all to see. We used crimson purple and it gave us a deep rose effect. Robin egg blue is also good.

If at any time, you wish a lighter color or background, you may add a little turpentine to the oil and mix them well. The more turpentine, the lighter the oil, and the lighter your background. Be sure you have good turpentine and your turpentine is not watery, as water will dry in spots and absorb no color. You are really better to choose a light powder. You can also blend different tints to a background. Apply your lighter color first and carry same slightly into the next part which is to be a little darker. Then on the edge of next color blend in, softening it as it approaches each edge. Never leave a sharp line. If you wish you can also give the background a light coat of flux or glaze to produce a more brilliant effect on dark greens or some blues. Never attempt to paint over or apply decals or gold to dry unfired ground.

You could also use matt colors or enamels, but matt colors are dull and enamels chip very easily.

Glaze paint for dry dusting gives you a lighter, airier color than regular.

Gold can be ground laid by applying first a coat of liquid bright gold and then applying the regular gold in powder form, much the same as you apply the color to the oil. This makes a good surface for agate etching, has a satin appearance and will show off the brilliancy of etching. Gold designs on the blue background show up beautifully.

After your china is fired, be sure to burnish your gold.

DRY DUSTING WITH DESIGNS

If you wish a design on your background, outline the design with china ink or stencil paste and let it dry. Then proceed with grounding instructions. As the powder will stick only where the oil is applied. It takes a day (24 hrs.) for a grounding coat to dry naturally and only if artificial heat is used can you hasten the process. You may also cut out a design on a dry background while the ground is fresh. Fire .016.

VELLUM FINISH

Mix vellum with china medium rather stiff, then thin with tinting oil. Mix well till it drops off the knife, in other words the paint must be thin. Use flat brush to apply. Work fast with it and it should be thinned enough to go on your surface very smooth like. Don't crisscross. Don't try to patch or build up. Should come out nice, smooth and satiny. Fire .016. Now you are ready to apply your decals and gold and fire again .016 on china.

MATTE FINISH

Matte colors are very easy to apply. The colors are opaque and have a velvet-like surface when fired. They can be prepared and applied just like any other china colors are but they are mostly used for backgrounds. They will stand firing without fading. Mix your matte color to a thin consistency, it will even out at once. Just paint it on, using a flat brush. Mix with medium and thin with tinting oil. Apply decals after it is fired.

It is not advisable to use matte colors on tableware or any other article that should be washed frequently. Matte colors retain grease, dust, etc. ,and would soon lose that delicate velvet color, which makes them lovely to look at.

NOTES

ENAMELING

Mix glaze with enamel medium, mix well. Mix 'till it is stringy and will drop in a string. This way it will pile in a little pile. Always scoop brush underneath the pile with a liner brush 00. Remember you never paint with enamels, you draw the strings of paint out and let the strings paint themselves. They are designed to lay on top of china. Your china should already have your design on in black. You always leave a little margin along the black line in between or colors will run together. Blow on paint to put moisture in once in awhile and also while mixing. Apply the paint heavy by line and fill in. Let it settle, don't daub back into the paint. Leave a center hole open in the flower for yellow dot. The black outline will not let paint run down if not applied too heavily.

When you mix white enamel with regular china colors, mix together well. First before putting enamel medium with it. Do not leave any turpentine in your brush that you clean and then put it in enamel paint or it will blister in firing. Use stroke of brush and flow on, it will leave a little pile that will level down. When it skins on top, stir it up (a drop of turpentine).

43

NOTES

CHAPTER FIVE

LOST ARTS
DECORATING CANDLES

Place in a muffin tin, in each compartment, a piece of parafin, the size of a large walnut. Then add one teaspoon of bronze powder, gold, crimson-gold, green gold, or copper gold. Each compartment a different color. Put more parafin in if needed to make a paint.

Warm and dissolve and stir parafin and bronze powder. Now take your candle you wish to decorate. Hold it by the wick, have your parafin hot (but not boiling) and take a teaspoon of one color of parafin and hold it against the candle at top and let it run down in a tear drop style, some long, some short tear drops. Do this with each color, blending the colors desired. Do this until the candle is completely covered but do not do the bottom. Now hang on tight wire with a clothespin until dry. Maybe 20 minutes.

Buy a good candle that won't limp with the weatherman. You can stretch a wire tightly across the room you are working in. These candles are beautiful and you will enjoy making the various combinations. Different colors of bronze powder may be purchased in dry form for this project.

BEADING LAMPSHADE
LOST ART

Choose the flower or design you like in a cretonne material. Choose lamp shade frame. Cut cretonne in pattern to cover shade.

First wrap frame with cloth tape before you start to cover it. Then you place cretonne on the shade tight. Should have a drum effect.

Second—You apply white shellac on cretonne on shade completely on the outside, four to five coats. Let coats dry first before you apply the next coat. Now you have the glassy effect.

Third—You apply the last coat of shellac, let it get tacky or sticky before you apply beads. Take a teaspoon of small glass beads (select colors of beads to match pattern colors) and apply the beads to that particular color. Take your time. Let it dry and do another part of the design the same way. Continue doing until your lampshade designs have been shellacked and glass beads added.

Suggestion: White beads all over a painted cretonne shade give a frosted effect and colors in cretonne will show through beautifully. Black cretonne, especially beautiful.

CHAMOIS PAINTING
LOST ART

Select a smooth chamois, holding it up to the light so as to be sure there are not thin places in it. Then press lightly on the smooth side with a cool iron. This makes the surface easier to paint on.

Take your oil paints out on a blotting paper and let them stand at least a day before using, to absorb the oil, then with a palette knife, place your paints

NOTES

on the palette to prepare the tints desired, adding a little mixing medium to thin and mix. In painting pale colors first paint with good white, to prevent the colors from sinking into the chamois. When entirely dry, paint in their natural colors in oil.

Be sure at first that you fasten your material and lightly sketch in design with dark paint or transfer by means of impression paper or stamped embroidery patterns. Use regular oil paints.

VELVET PAINTING

Use regular oil paints. To thin use a little mixing medium. The golden rod makes a beautiful design for a screen painted on black or dark shade of velvet and is easy to make. Put your paints out on a blotting paper for a day before. Make your cloth secure with thumb tacks.

SILK OR SATIN PAINTNG FOR DRESSES OR PILLOWS

Fasten a piece of blotting paper over a drawing board, then put powdered soapstone over it (buy from any drugstore). Now you fasten the silk or satin to be painted over it and make it secure with thumb tacks.

Take your oil paints out on a blotting paper and let them remain at least a day before using to absorb the oil, then with your knife place them back on your palette. After painting let it remain until wholly dry, it will absorb the oil. Now you will notice a little of the powder remaining on the wrong side, when first removed, but it will easily brush off. Remember let your paints set out a day on blotting paper to absorb the oil. Use regular artists oils. Sketch your design in with white paint on dark material or black paint on light material, or stamped, as for embroidery work.

After you have drawn your design on your material and the material is fastened with thumb tacks to your drawing board, mix a small quantity of the color desired with the medium about as thick as cream. Mix only a few colors at a time. Stir with your brush before using as the medium dries rapidly. If too thick, add a little turpentine. Use bristle brushes for velvet or plush and for silk or satin, use camel hair brushes. Always remember to try to take long dragging strokes in your painting. In painting the velvet type materials, always draw the brush down in the same direction the nap goes. Apply the paint thickly and lightly, and commence at the outer edge and work toward the center of your leaves and flowers. If you are painting light flowers paint first with white, after it dries, then color or use your metallic colors.

After your work is thoroughly dry, if desired, you may outline in gold or silver.

NOTES

CHAPTER SIX

LUSTRE COLORS AND EFFECTS

Many years I have spent experimenting with different combinations of lustres and their colors. In this chapter are some of the colors combined and their results plus the art of application.

Lustre painting is beautiful and very interesting. On small vases or plates, one can produce some very nice work.

To begin, lustres are always in liquid form and look very much alike in this state. Always keep your bottle closed and never forget and switch corks or tops of one bottle to another. Try to have a different brush for each color lustre for best results. Now let us be sure our work area is clean, we have plenty of room and the proper supplies are on hand.

Our china, square shading brush, turpentine, alcohol, oil of lavendar, lustre, lambs wool, silk material to make a dabber.

If your lustre has congealed, remove a small amount of lustre with a palette knife that has been cleaned with denatured alcohol. Put it on a piece of glass that has been cleaned with alcohol. Now regrind the lustre with lustre essence or lavender oil to the usual consistency. Remember I stress cleanliness.

First clean the china thoroughly, even using alcohol (blemishes and spots on fired lustres are caused by dust on the plate or brush or by dampness, turpentine, handling or in the kiln). Now take the shade of lustre you desire for the first coat and apply with a large square shader ½″ brush (flat) (fine hair). The fewer the strokes, the smoother will be the effect. Now did you get it on too heavy, better rub it off, as your alcohol will remove the unfired lustres and re-apply. If you put on your lustres properly they will not have to be padded. Everything depends on your consistency of your lustre and a good flat lustre brush and your speed.

If you wish you can use your little silk dabber. Work swiftly, apply a small amount of the oil of lavander to the dabber as lustres dry quickly. (This will give it a little slower drying and the padding will be more successful). Dab evenly to pick up heavy deposits you may have made and the dabbing will blend brush marks or surplus out and make the china more uniform in appearance.

If you have the inside of cups or pitchers, they can be processed by poring a small quantity of lustre into them and rubbing it around with a silk dabber or brush. To cover all the surface or maybe just over a design, as you desire it. Work fast and when pad starts to feel sticky stop, for the lustre will start pulling off. It is now ready for fire. Since it is freshly applied, dry them well by artificial heat and wrap the pieces in thin paper as cloth or cotton will stick and cause blemishes. Keep in a dry place and fire as soon as possible. (Moisture will show up after firing in white places in the finished lustre). Fire .16 on china.

Now you have fired your china and should you desire other colors apply the color desired and repeat the same way and fire again. To produce the even tints, re-apply the lustre for several firings but never attempt to apply an extra coat over an unfired coat (as the unfired lustre would soften and expand and the result would be a blotched effect). Spotty lustre can be corrected by re-applying the same color or covering

NOTES

it with a darker coat tint. Also by covering the faulty part with a coat of mother of pearl. White has no tint. It is used for rubbing off colors or over light tints, like rose, yellow, light green to produce a pearl effect. If your lustre comes out of firing too light, re-apply same and refire.

Enamels applied over unfired lustre will take a pinkish tone and some very good combinations will be pleasing to you.

Gold applied over unfired lustre will lose its brilliancy and will fire half matt. Paste may be used over unfired lustre, if it is very dry. But better results, if it is fired before applying the paste.

Lustre applied over India ink will fire off. Gold must be always burnished before applying lustre over the gold, or the colors will give poor results. If orange has crackle, you can apply a coat of yellow and fire again. This should correct the trouble. Holes appearing in fired lustre, shows dirt, re-lustre and fire again.

STENCILING CHINA

A design on lustre is made by drawing a fine stencil design with china pencil or fire in a very light or simple decal. Mix your stencil powder with water to make a brushing consistency. Use a soft pointed brush or a pointed toothpick. Apply this stencil paste to your design. See that your pattern is perfect. Let it dry for about 30 minutes. Apply lustre and paint over design and all of plate. Do not go back over more than once. Do not leave shadows or bubbles. Do not shake lustre. Use lustre essence to thin. Always work from outside in. Fire and apply second coat of whatever you desire. Your stencil powder will fire away, leaving the design you put on. See color design 3.

LUSTRE EFFECTS OVER WHITE CHINA

Rich Maroon can be made by covering one application of liquid bright silver with one or two applications of purple or ruby. This effect is very rich and will make a splendid border for paste and gold, or also an all-over rich color for a small piece.

Auburn Iridescent is produced by applying a coating of *yellow pearl over the already fired orange lustre.* This effect makes a very effective lining for small pieces and produces good results in combination with different designs. A good color for nut bowls, conventional small pieces, etc.

Iridescent Blue, strong and beautiful, is made by

covering copper bronze with pearl lustre. This is a very striking effect, of the nature of peacock green.

Semi-Matt Black, nearly iridescent, is made by applying pearl lustre over a fired coat of regular mineral black paint. The effect is very useful for a large background and in combination with other designs in pure lustres.

Tiger Lily effect can be obtained with an uneven application of violet lustre applied from top down and leaving long narrow white spots. When fired, apply a generous coating of yellow pearl covering the whole. This color is effective for small vases or jugs.

Pigeon Iridescent is very pretty and useful for lining, can be made with one application of pigeon lustre. Apply it carefully and notice the pretty effect.

Gold Sheen is obtained by covering pigeon grey pearl over a fired coat of liquid bright gold.

Mahogany Iridescent is made by applying ruby unevenly on the first firing, possibly leaving small parts of china untouched and giving a generous coating of yellow pearl on the successive firing, covering everything.

Green Iridescent Can be Made by One Application, or perhaps two, of green pearl. This color will fire better and make a more delicate lining than all other greens, because it's tint is very light and pearly.

Royal Dark Blue is made by one or possibly two applications of dark blue. This color is very good for plate borders.

Combination: A background of yellow brown lustre worked up in gold lustre ornaments will make a very rich set. It must be remembered that gold lustre is a strong maroon.

Green Iridescent is obtained by applying a generous coat of pearl over an already fired blue green.

Bronzy Effects quite odd and good are obtained by applying yellow pearl over a fired coat of liquid bright silver. This tint looks much like an old bronze Roman effect.

Semit-Glaze Crystal effect has been obtained by applying yellow pearl over fired bright gold. This effect will work well in connection with olive green or finishing brown and gold for cups, bowls, small jars, etc.

Dark Russian Green is obtained from two applications of dark green and one of brilliant green. This green tint is very rich and transparent.

Lemon Gold can be made by covering fired liquid bright gold with mother of pearl. This effect is rather startling, but looks well on small pieces with an uneven surface.

NOTES

Yellow Pearl Gives a Very Pretty Effect. Its tone is full of iridescence in greenish and yellows and produces beautiful effects. Combines well with gold designs.

Shamoy Shell is made with one application of orange fired over rose.

Greenish Brown is made with one light coat of olive green. Use this special color very light to prevent crackling.

Strong Steel effect is produced by applying blue lustre over fired gold.

Beautiful Metallic is made with one application of green pearl over a fired coating of brilliant green.

Peacock Green can be produced by an application of dark green or brilliant green, or light green over one fired coating of copper bronze lustre. This color has in itself the beautiful dark iridescence of the peacock color and makes a good ground for paste and gold.

Iridescent Silver can be made with a coating of liquid bright silver on the first firing and one of pigeon grey pearl, carelessly applied on the second.

Peacock Blue is made by applying liquid bright gold on the first firing and one or two coats of dark green. The iridescent effect of this color, when successfully obtained, is very beautiful.

Warm Shell effect is made by covering a fired coat of rose with a light coating of yellow. This shell tone makes a fine decoration for small pieces like salts, saucers, trays, etc., applied in the all-over fashion.

Deep Bluish tone is produced by covering with blue the already fired violet lustre. This tint makes a beautiful tone for borders and combines well with paste and gold decorations.

Apple Green uneven and nearly iridescent is made by applying yellow over fired pigeon grey pearl. It can also be made with one light and padded coating of brilliant green. The appearance of the latter will then be an even delicate green.

Copper Red is done by applying copper over fired black. The black tone underneath seems to help in developing the copper red of the last application.

Combination: Trees or foliage in dark green intermixed with other in orange will make a striking combination.

Purplish Bronze is obtained by covering a rich coat of fired Roman gold with orange lustre. Apply this latter unevenly.

Dark Tiffany Effect, much similar to the effect produced on Tiffany glass: can be made by applying one rich application of Roman gold, and on the second firing, one of dark green lustre. The bronzy tones made with this combination are very beautiful and decorative in small bowls, jars, etc.

Light Tiffany sheen effect is produced with one rich application of Roman gold and one or two of light green lustre on the successive firings. A good effect is made by applying (over fired gold) long strokes of light and dark green intermixed, possibly leaving some very small touches of gold uncovered.

Opal lustre is similar to mother of pearl, only more whitish. It is used often in place of the latter tint and its effects are always very attractive. Opal will fade away if fired too strongly.

Brownish Red is made by covering fired violet with a light coating of yellow lustre. This gives a peculiar effect, sometimes nearly iridescent.

Pleasing Effect: Large designs in flowers or foliage painted in yellow, on a background of dark brown, will produce a pleasing decoration.

Meissen Brown Pearl is obtained by one application of yellow pearl over a coating of orange.

Strong Metallic red can be made by applying rose over fired liquid bright gold.

Reddish Tones are obtained by applying yellow over fired copper bronze.

Grey Green is made with a light application of light green lustre. If padded this color will nearly disappear and show a brownish light tint. It should therefore be applied light and without padding so as to obtain a grey green effect.

Frosty Silver is made by covering some decorations or grounds made with regular mineral china color, with silver lustre.

Black tint is produced with at least two applications of black lustre. It is not possible to make with lustres, the dense black made with the mineral colors. By repeated applications, however, a solid blackish tone will be obtained.

Delicate sheen effect is produced by covering antique gold with pearl lustre.

Yellow Green: The nearest tone to yellow green can be made with one or two applications of brilliant green lustre. This color is brightest of all the greens.

Deep Blue Green tint is made with one or possibly two coatings of blue green lustre.

(Combination:) An all-over design in yellow large chrysanthemums made with yellow pearl painted on a background of black, either lustre or powder, will make a striking effect.

NOTES

Light Blue is made with a light application of turquoise blue or blue grey. A ground of the above tints looks very pretty in combination with enamels and a touch of gold. Apply the lustre, fire ,and then apply the enamels.

Shading Green can better be produced by two applications of dark green. The more the applications the more even and darker will be the effect.

Poppy or Yellow Red cannot be made with lustre color. One application of ruby covered with yellow will however give a strong reddish tone.

Primrose Yellow is made with one application or more of yellow lustre. Yellow lustre is very pretty tint for linings and often gives a slightly iridescent effect. This color is also useful when applied over different other lustres, as will be found on these pages.

Splendid Effects can be obtained by covering in part a piece with long artistic strokes with copper bronze in the fashion of ornaments, leaving small spaces plain white. On the second firing cover the whole with brilliant green and notice the beautiful result.

Good Combination is made by decorating a bowl, etc., with dark blue, leaving plain white spaces in the shape of small apple blossoms. On the second firing cover the whole with pigeon lustre. The flowers must be in large quantities. A black outline will improve it greatly.

Good Decoration of small vases, plaques, etc., will be made by applying well drawn ornaments in brilliant green. The more of these the prettier the effect. On the second firing these ornaments may be outlined in black or gold.

Iridescent Rose is made with the color of this name. It's tint is rather purplish and not always successful.

Light Green Over Copper Bronze gives a strong metallic, similar to peacock green.

Figure: Figures can be painted in lustre effectively when in a conventional style. Broad dark outlines of the figures should be fired at first, and the lustre tints afterwards. The nearest tint to flesh would be brown lustre applied flat and very thin. The draperies can be painted in almost any of the lustre tints.

Olive Green lustre is a brownish and uneven tint. If used lightly, the effect will be pretty and almost iridescent. In combination with gold flowers and outlining this color makes a good tint for nut bowls.

Silver Ornaments: A scroll of silver luster over a background of dark blue lustre looks very rich and makes a very fine decoration for small sets, or vases. The scrolls should be broad and in long lines. Liquid bright silver is also good for this work.

Pretty Effects of Flowers Can Be Made by Covering a border or a broad ground with dark green or light green, leaving small spaces plain white. On these apply carefully little roses in rose lustre. On the second firing the stems and small leaves can be applied.

Odd Effects can be made by designing a small piece with flowers and ornaments in Roman gold. Also with trees or birds, filling nearly all your china. On the next firing cover your gold in part, say the flowers with orange, and the leaves with dark green, or in some odd way, leaving only small lines of gold. The effect will be bronzy, odd and artistic.

Realistic Subjects can easily be painted with lustre colors. Use violet for violets, rose for light roses, ruby for dark roses, black for blackberries, yellow for yellow flowers, brilliant green and dark green for the leaves. The shading for these subjects can be applied on the second firing. With a black outline these flowers will be much improved.

Landscape: Paint long pine trees and broader trees in piegon grey pearl, from the top down, covering the largest part of a tall little vase. The sky should be in yellow pearl. This effect can be made in one firing (if carefully applied) and makes a pleasing decoration, looking like a delicate sunset.

Marine Landscape: Make a complete background, sky and water of pearl lustre. Put a light horizon line of pigeon grey, and paint a boat in the foreground with regular china paints. The whole effect will be transparent and pretty for small tall vases.

Conventional Decorations are easily made with lustre colors. Apply your designs flat, one near the other, allowing the first ones to dry well before applying the second. On the successive firing outline your subjects.

Yellow Brown tint is made with one application of the lustre bearing this name. This tint will make a pretty band for bowls or saucers, etc., and works well in combination with gold.

Meissen Brown Tint can be produced with two coatings of brown lustre.

Strong Contrasts, but new and good ones, can be obtained by covering a tall narrow vase or a candlestick with yellow pearl and on the second firing covering parts of it with small ornaments in gold.

Blue Iridescent is made with one covering of pearl over copper bronz.

Yellow Brown Shell can be made by applying a coating of rose lustre on the first firing and covering it in small parts with orange and other small parts with yellow on the second. This intermixing of the last two colors will make a pretty effect.

NOTES

Shading Green tint can also be obtained by covering a coating of steel blue with yellow lustre.

Bluish and Purple Hues are made by applying yellow over fired black lustre.

Orange is made with lustre bearing this name. Apply it in two very light coatings. If too thick this color crackles or chips off.

Ivory Yellow is made with one very light and possibly a padded coating of yellow lustre. Pad it evenly.

Dark Green can be produced with two applications of dark green lustre. Very often one coating of this color will produce a light tone. Repeat until the right tone is obtained.

Strong Brick Red is made with a covering of orange over fired ruby lustre. However, this effect is not pleasing unless it is worked over with gold designs or heavy black lines.

Ruby Lustre can be obtained with two light coatings of ruby. If this special color is applied thick it's brilliancy will be lost. Use light and repeat.

Violet Lustre is produced with the lustre so named. It's tone is rich and is very appropriate for borders.

Mother of Pearl is made by applying a coat of the color of that name. Apply it carelessly and do not pad it. This is one of the most popular colors and makes a beautiful lining for cups, saucers, bowls, jars, trays, etc.

Strong Violet is also made with an application of ruby over dark blue lustre.

Good Decorations are made with an all-over floral design in dark blue lustre. Perhaps a little outlining in gold would be more striking. This effect is very appropriate for coat of arms, on plaques or steins and tankards, also tiles, producing an artistic decoration. We do not intend to limit this effect to the above shapes.

Shell Effect for fish sets or lining is made with mother of pearl or iridescent applied in a careless way. A number of shells and corals surrounded by these pearls make a fine combination and a very effective fish set. Green pearl would also make a good background for a fish set.

Gold Lustre: This color is a beautiful, rich dark maroon and fires dark in one coating. This is probably one of the richest purplish tones in the lustres.

Many Other Effects can be obtained by using the different lustre colors as a broad, plain, all over ground. Ruby gold lustre, copper bronz, browns, pearls, greens, etc., make a beautiful ground. The most artistic decorations however, are those made of repeated designs and combinations of tints applied in harmonious effect.

From the combinations given on these pages, the decorators will find suggestions for new ideas and new colors, and the ambitious experimenter will find this branch of painting very interesting and full of surprises.

(Lustre colors can easily be altered by adding thinning oil or oil of lavender. These colors will not give satisfactory results and the decorator should use good judgment in selecting reliable materials).

Scarlet: Apply orange lustre over ruby.

Deep Bluish Violet Tone: Two applications of black lustre, covered by a third coat of ruby lustre.

Deep Iridescent Green: One coat of ruby lustre, then apply a coat of dark or light green lustre.

Gold Spray Designs beautiful over black lustres.

Yellow: Used for backgrounds or a stronger yellow is desired. Apply and refire it a number of times.

Brown: Good color for banding and if desired— outline.

DON'TS FOR LUSTRE

Turpentine must not be left in brush after cleaning.

Finger marks will show when handling a lustre tinted piece.

Don't use cotton or tissues around wet lustre.

Never breathe on your work or cough. Moisture will show up in firing.

Don't try to mix or blend lustres.

Don't use the same brush in different color lustres.

Never leave your bottles uncorked.

Never switch corks or tops of one bottle to another.

Don't apply thick or it will crackle off.

Do not apply orange lustre too thick, it will also crackle off.

Underfired lustres will rub off.

Don't rub over lustre while burnishing gold, it is easily scratched.

DO FOR LUSTRE

Clean brushes before use, first with Turpentine and then alcohol.

Dry your brushes thoroughly.

NOTES

Use essence of lustre or oil of lavender for thinning.

Use lint free cloth and denatured alcohol where needed.

Put cotton over lambs wool pad and then silk over both. Tie, for dabber.

Do fire and paint again for deeper coats.

Do apply one coat over the other of different colors after they have been fired.

Do remove fired lustre with liquid china eraser.

Do apply the lustre in the last firing over china painting or decal.

Do warm your china lightly, and lustre will go on more evenly.

REMEMBER

Cleanliness — Lightness — Thin Coats
Are Your Three Rules To Lustre Painting

Tea Jar: Outline design in black. Background with light green lustre, fire. Second, go over background with dark green lustre. Do leaves, stems and caps of flower in light green lustre. Flowers and buds in yellow lustre. Fire. Beautiful.

NOTES

CHAPTER SEVEN

FLOWER SUGGESTIONS

Narcissus: Light yellow and apple green, center yellow brown, yellow red and a little yellow — leaves yellow green, brown green or shading green — little apple green.

Tulips: Pink — rose, shaded with blood red and mauve. White — apple green — pale and rose, shade a little down with yellows. Stems — apple green. Leaves — yellow green, shading green and brown green.

Freesia: Wash of light yellow, little apple green and dash of mauve. Stems — shading green and black. Leaves — yellow green and brown green.

Trumpet Narcissus: Light yellow, albert yellow, yellow brown. Centers are yellow brown and yellow red. Leaves are moss green, shading green.

Tube Rose: Brown green and mauve shaded with apple green and rose. Centers yellow. Leaves — yellow green and shading green. Stems — apple green and mauve.

Cherry Blossom: Leaves — apple green, yellow green and shading green. Blossoms are shaded with apple green and little rose. Stamens are albert yellow and brown green.

Haw Apples: Yellow red and blood red, shaded with blood red and violet and a little brown. Cap — blood red and auburn or dark brown.

Blue Berries: Sea green and deep blue green, shade with banding blue, sea green and Copenhagen blue.

Gourd: Leaves—grey green and two-toned. Flower — soft yellow, yellow ochre and albert yellow.

Miner's Lettuce Flower: Leaves — moss green, gray yellow, yellow brown and violet of iron. Stems are more violet of iron. Flowers — use light pompadour. Center of little units and lower leaves are ruby.

California Poppy: Lemon yellow and shade with brown green and yellow brown to warm up. Stamens are yellow brown and brown green. Leaves are apple green and lemon yellow. Stems same and shading green.

Hollyhock: Flowers — yellow and pompadour shading towards center with blood red. Leaves — apple green and brown green. Stems — same and little mauve.

Lady Slipper: Violet and grey flesh. Leaves — shading green and apple green. Last firing — apple green and violet.

Mission Bell Flower: Thin wash of yellow shaded with yellow brown. Center of flower is yellow with a little brown green. Stamens are yellow red. Stems are moss green and little yellow. Leaves are moss green and grey flesh.

Fairy Lanterns, Wild: Leaves are apple green and shading green. Stems are brown green and shading green. Flowers are mauve and a little apple green. Highlights are white. On second fire paint thin wash of yellow over flowers.

REMEMBER—Do not lose track of the center of your flower. If the center looks nice, the flower will

NOTES

look good. Make a good eye in center. Begin with a dot or a few dots and work out.

ROSES — *American Beauty:* Paint the dark center and broad mass of shadow in crimson purple, mix with 1/6 part of darkest green. Paint half shadows with pure crimson purple and leave the lighter parts plain white. Fire. Now wash over shadows with crimson purple and light parts with American beauty color. Detail petals with crimson purple. Fire. Then retouch with same colors and fire.

If black or brown is mixed with purples, they will oxidize faster than if dark green or peacock green are used.

Pink Roses: Use crabapple pink or rose carmine, a little pompadour center. A soft effect is produced by dusting a little brown green toward the shadow part of the rose before the second fire. Keep centers pure rose. Rose, pink and peach will chip off if color is put on too thick. Leaves are grape green and apple green.

White Roses: Shadows painted either grey or ashes of roses or a mixture of black and blue. Center — a pink or yellow brown tone. Center can be dusted when dry. Keep the shadows even and light and paint the rose in one color, and if possible dust a little.

Yellow Rose: Brown green for the shadows and yellow brown for the center.

Poppies, Field: Use poppy red or yellow red in the lighter places and violet of iron for the shadows. Center — Dark green with little black dots.

Violets: Violet, red violet and royal violet and tints can be mixed a little with banding blue to make the color more bluish or ruby, whichever will give a warmer purplish cast to the violet. Equal part of ruby and banding blue make a good violet. Or two parts of violet of yellow brown. Make your petal in one stroke, it will look better. If you need a darker tone use a little black.

Daffodils: Light brown green. Shadow in the center with light yellow brown leaving highlights white. Fire. Then wash petals with light lemon yellow and center with egg yellow.

Forget-Me-Nots: Use deep blue green or turquoise blue.

Wisteria: Orchid violet, heliotrope and lilac anglo. Leaves — grey green and brown green.

Grapes: Banding blue shaded with blue black and ruby. Highlight. Fire. Leaves — yellow green shaded with olive green. Touches of yellow brown and blood red. Background — ivory yellow, light tint.

Acorns: Finishing brown, chestnut brown, albert yellow. Leaves — finishing brown, sepia brown, red brown and moss green in lightest parts, dark leaves same

color, only darker. A little Copenhagen blue under chestnuts is pretty. On the last fire dust with a little finishing brown.

Brodiae: Flowers, thin wash yellow shaded in center with apple green and in center with strong yellow. Leaves — apple green, shading green and touch of black. Stems are yellow and apple green.

Verbena: Light yellow shaded with yellow brown and brown green. Center — yellow red. Leaves — brown green and yellow brown. Stems — yellow brown and black.

Verbena, Pink: Flowers — rose. Center — yellow. Leaves — moss green annd brown green. Stems — blood red and mauve.

Bittersweet: Outline berries with blood red or poppy red and fire. Then paint berries with yellow red, shade with blood red. Leaves — yellow brown and moss green and brown green. Stems — auburn brown. Highlight berries. Deep purple for shading leaves.

Chrysanthemum: Light side of flower with a wash of lemon yellow, then yellow brown and albert yellow for shading. Deepest shadows are yellow brown and brown green and blood red. Leaves — moss green and yellow green and brown green and shading green.

Petunia, Varigated: Banding blue and violet, ruby purple toward center. Center, use brown green and yellow brown. Veinings in flowers are blood red and violet. Stems — yellow brown and brown green. Leaves — brown green and moss green. Buds are paler than flower.

Also rose purple — carmine purple.

Gladiolus: Thin carnation toward center, blood red and little ruby. Buds are a little deeper. Leaves are apple green and yellow. Shading — green and little yellow brown.

Bachelor's Button: Flowers banding blue and deep blue, green for paler ones. Center—Copenhagen blue and violet. Leaves — apple green and shading green. Stems—shading green. Some flowers will be Copenhagen blue and banding blue.

Phlox: Leaves back of flower yellow green and shading green and black light parts shading green, apple green, yellow green. Flowers are white and some light apple green and violet for shadows. Some flowers Copenhagen blue and violet. Centers—touch of yellow and blood red. Some flowers deep rose pink, using wash blood red with a little violet. Centers are blood red.

Nasturtiums: Flowers — lemon yellow and blood red, albert yellow, yellow brown, yellow red, orange

NOTES

yellow and ivory. Center — lemon yellow. Leaves and stems are olive green and a little light yellow.

Japanese Lantern Plant: Leaves — yellow green and brown green and shading green. Stems — brown green and violet. Lanterns — yellow and apple green. Yellow green for shading and veining the lantern stems. Shading — green and black.

Cherries: Lemon yellow, yellow red and blood red. For dark cherries, cherry red, maroon and shade with pansy purple. Unripe cherries — use yellow green and shade it into yellow red. Stems — apple green shaded with violet of iron. Woody stems are brown green, dark brown and Copenhagen grey for highlights.

Tulips: First fire, blood red with carnation for highlights and ruby for shadows, or you can use blood red and pompadour for the first fire and blood red for the second fire. The flower should be kept red or streaked with yellow, as red near gold intensifies the brilliancy of both. Yellow background is good. Leaves — equal parts shading brown, green and should have a kind of bluish cast. Touch parts and tips with light brown a little.

Wild Roses: Rosebud, carmine. Centers — albert yellow. Stamen and stem of sepia brown. Leaves and body of delicate green lettuce. Seed pods bright red. Background combined Russian green and cream ivory and green at base and blend in dark with light.

Daisies: Centers lemon yellow, darker touches egg yellow, delicate shading of grey in flowers. Background oriental blue at top and blend down with lemon yellow and red brown.

Water Lily (white): Shade the flowers with egg yellow and brown green and shading green. Leaves — yellow green and brown green. Stamen — egg yellow and yellow red. Background — between very light tint of may green.

Currants: Backgrounds — blend apple green, violet of iron and brown at bottom and over handle, and blue and yellow at top. Blend all colors into each other. Flush also over some of leaves after it is fired first time. Apple green and brown green mixed in right proportions will make pretty handles for cups and vases when same colors are used in design. This eliminates so much gold.

Fuchsias: For pink one use rose color. For purple centers use violet of gold and deep blue mixed together. Yellow and orange for your petals. For stems light brown, orange and pink. Shade leaves with deep chrome green and light brown.

Fern: Mixing yellow, chrome green and a little light brown.

Coffee Berries: For blossoms use blue, orange and rose mixed for centers. Ruby with a small dot of mixing yellow. For berries — capucine red, ruby or deep purple. Jonquil yellow, apple green and orange yellow. For the leaves and stems shading green, orange yellow and albert yellow.

Honeysuckle: Capucine red for the flowers and centers of mixing yellow. Stems and Leaves — use yellow brown, apple green and brown. On the second fire shade flowers with ruby and centers with orange.

SALMON COLOR FOR TINTING — 2 parts of tillet or capucine red, one part orange, ½ of rose and a small amount of flux as rose color. Grind in tinting oil.

Strawberries: Yellow red and pompadour. Seeds are made with touches of chestnut brown. Unripe berries are painted with mixing yellow and yellow green shaded into pompadour red. Berries in background may be shaded with Copenhagen grey and tinted with yellow and a little pompadour red. Leaves are painted with olive green, brown green, dark green, Meissen brown and touches of pompadour red. Background of brown tones such as egg yellow shaded into chestnut brown and darkened with deep red brown in darkest tones are nice.

Geraniums: Rose and the darker ones with brown pink. Wipe out highlights. Fire. Second firing retouch with carnation, blood red and pompadour red. Leaves are yellow green, olive green and brown green. Reddish tint in the leaves is produced by blending in crimson, violet of gold, auburn brown and a little shading brown in the shadows.

A softness in flowers may be made by powdering with carnation, use it sparingly. Darker flowers may be powdered with brown, pink and pompadour red which may be blended into a background of lemon yellow, shaded into egg yellow, yellow brown, and sunburn brown. Blend a little apple green into the yellow and it will add more life.

NOTES

CHAPTER EIGHT

FOR A BIRD PLATE

Arrange birds anywhere on the plate, 10" or 12", like they are sitting in a tree (as you will be painting a tree in later). I use the lovebirds. About seven or eight. Fire decals in on china .016. Now draw your tree and branches so the birds will have something to sit on. You will also find decals with a few tree blossoms or small leaves to put on your trees. Let your plate dry. Pad in your sky, using azure blue, elargo rose, and a little albert yellow, blue on top—blending down to the bottom with yellow. Trees are dark brown and black green. Part of tree may stem from another tree not seen. Touch up your birds with a little paint also. Band edge of plate if desired.

SQUARE PLATE

You may use flowers in china indentation or leave plain. Use a figure design in the middle or a flower design. But circle your picture in the center with a band of gold. Scroll and emboss your gold work in and edge your gold on plate with finger. (See Filigree Chapter). DESIGN 1

HORSES

Put your favorite horse in middle of plate, 10" preferred, for this design. Around edge of plate put small horses, or riding horses, as illustrated and jockey caps under these horses. Fire.

Second—Connect up your decals around edge. I used brown green and black green to connect our decals of horses around edge, making it look like grass. Then take your design pattern and make a scroll dip edge on this plate. Fire. DESIGN 10

BALLOON PLATE

Here we are at the park. Balloons in the sky. People watching in the park. After you have applied these decals make a few pathways for the bicycle, bicycle rider or the horse back rider, as well as the carriage. Don't be afraid to get up your decals for this. All decals in. Dry and fire.

Second—Touch up your decals with color needed. Sky will be azure blue glaze. Glaze must be ground good, so thin it will run from knife in drops and after you dip pad in paint, dab sky lightly. You will have other colors in background and have different pads for different color paints. When you form a cloud, remember the inside of cloud is supposed to be darker. For white clouds take padded stick and wipe out inside instead of painting inside. If you care not for the balloons, try airplanes. They could also be watching an airplane show or???

Now be sure you have joined together the park scene with a few strokes of grass or walks or something, so that it looks like a large enjoyable park. Finger band of gold is fine on this. DESIGN 11

NOTES

DOG PLATE

Use Meissen design (preferred) beagle dog or any dog you like. Place in center of plate. Apply your scenery views around the dog. Now visualize the dog standing out in the field near the edge of a water inlet. As this is not an island in the sky you see on the plate but a small island. Your water in this inlet is a little darker than your sky. After you have your decals all on, fire (china .016).

Second—To connect your decals on your ground. Pad in yellow brown and blend in and pad light and heavy. Then take your brush and blotch a little to make your field look like grain or dry weeds. Pad (blue glaze) sky, blotch a little to make a cloud. Make your water a little darker, blotch it a little to give life to the water. Use capucine brown or chocolate red brown to connect picture and olive green to touch up decals, where needed. Also to put in a little grass. Carry design of each decal to join other decals and gather together as if everything is in the one field. Make band plain or scroll in gold as desired.

When you are working on your plates, be in no hurry. By putting in some colors today and tomorrow or the next day, put in a few more. They will not run, neither will you be baking your plate away. Work on some other work. The more you can do with your plate before firing the second time, the better. *DESIGN 6*

JAPANESE or MIKADO GARDEN PLATE

Take a ten-inch plate or equal and a six-inch Mikado figure. Follow chapter on Decal Center Designs. Immerse your watermount decal as per instructions and place in the center of circle, face up. (Should you use the varnish decal, place in the center of circle face down).

Around the Mikado figure, use two pagodas, one small Japanese and cherry blossom and one large Japanese house, four small trees of Japanese style. These will come from your Japanese scenery sheet. This should now begin to look like a picture. Fire .016 on china.

Step 2. After firing, draw in lakes to join sandhills with china pencil. Pad in sandhills, using yellow brown. Pad in azure blue glaze for the lakes. After you have padded in blue, let this dry a minute and brush mark a little to create water looking like water. Touch up each color to accentuate decal design. The trees with olive green, black or capucine brown for the shadows and lines. If desired you can make a few birds in the air by making round M.

Now put a band of gold around your center Mikado picture and you are now ready to do one row of filagree of gold work. On the inside of circle is good. Also use crimson purple for the gown of some figures of the Mikado. Apply gold to edge of plate, either by finger, machine or neatly draw a design on edge with china pencil and apply your gold. Let dry and fire .016. After firing, polish gold as per chapter on Kulp's Roman gold. *DESIGN 15*

GROUP OF PLATES

These patterns are presented to show you about arranging many decals on the plates. The violet plate is especially pretty with its band of brown green instead of gold band. Gives the plate balance. It is especially beautiful when arranging flowers on a plate to paint gold in solid from the flowers to the edge of the plate, half way around the plate, blending out the line to an edge applied by finger the rest of the way. The gold will look beautiful when polished. The more you use Kulp's Roman gold color the better you will like it. *DESIGN 5*

PITCHER AND CUPS or MUGS

On our pitcher we have used the Brown eyed Susan flowers. But any pretty flower you like is fine. Then we applied our gold on the edge. Makes a beautiful set. *DESIGN 9*

MYTHS BY BACCHUS

A 10½ plate is selected. Any decal of your choice may be used. Place your decal in center of plate. Divide your border of the plate in five points. Use your pattern and lightly sketch a semi-circle around edge as shown. Place the large gold rose in this circle. Trim a small rose off so it will fit and add it in another spot. Remember roses grow upwards. Do not place your flowers upside down. In each triangle and below each large gold rose, place a single gold rose. Now if all decals are on, dry your plate and fire at .016.

After firing, color your fired decal with colors appearing in the decal (if desired). You accentuate your shadows and give your picture more life. Then place a band of gold around the decal in the center of the plate and a band of gold about 1½″ from the gold band around the center decal. Use your pattern to mark your semi-circles and paint the gold on the semi-circles. See your chapter on serventing and fill in as per picture. Band edge of plate with gold and Fire .016. We mention gold but remember we always use our mixture of Kulp's Roman Gold. *DESIGN 13*

NOTES

THE PHEASANT MEAT PLATTER

(Optional) Ground lay a ⅛" band around edge of meat platter with green and fire in.

Now—Place large pheasant picture in middle of plate. Place about 14 or what you need, according to size of meat platter, of two inch wildlife decals assorted pictures, around edge placing them every 1¼" apart. In between these small decals place a gold rose near top of plate. Fire.

2. Now place a circle of gold around the edge of each small circle. A ring of gold around the large pheasant. Follow serpentine effect between small decals and around edge. Where necessary darken your trees or shadows with capucine brown. Touch up green with olive green and yellow green, where needed, to bring out life to your colors and pictures. Now on the large pheasant decal, put in some grass, wild, high grass, as you wish to create a small swamp-like effect, using capucine brown and black green. A little blue water, maybe a lily pad and a marshy effect. Edge plate in gold. We always speak of just gold, but understand, we use exclusively Kulp's Roman gold formula. It will wear for years and is not gaudy looking.

THE MURILLO PLATE OR SOMETIMES CALLED BEGGAR BOYS

Use a 10" plate. Follow decal center design instructions. Now you will need five small and one 6" large Murillo decals. Place the large Murillo decal in center, place smaller Murillo decals around edge. Use five small gold roses below small decals and five larger gold roses in between as per pattern. Fire.

2. With your banding wheel or equal, place a ¼" band of gold around large Murillo decal and around edge of plate. Around the small Murillo decals, place a smaller (⅜") band and also ⅜" band to join each small decal. Now serpentine around your roses. Fire, .016. *DESIGN 4*

BLUE BOY VASE AND FLOWER VASE

Place a large decal on each side of vase (17th Century scenes romance of love and youth by Fragonard and are now obtainable for this vase). There are four designs. Now select the flowers you would like to use. Keep design of your flowers heavier on the bottom of the base, makes your top of vase look lighter. Have the flowers growing up to the top of vase. Fire.

2. Put band of gold at bottom. Draw scroll design at top and fill in with gold. Fire and polish. Get used to using your mixture of Roman gold and liquid gold and you will like it better all the time.

Place blue boy or similar large design on one side and pink lady on other side. Connect your decals together with fine line. Fire.

2. Put background in brown green at bottom then higher on the vase, use a little yellow, rose and blue. Yellow green glaze on top of vase and fire.

3. On each side of vase, draw a tree and limbs and leaves or choose a decal of trees. Use capucine brown and yellow green and brown green. Touch up colors in your fired decals. Put gold around base and draw a design and put in gold around neck of vase. Gold handles and fluted top. Fire and polish. Don't forget to blend and connect in your design, like they were standing on the ground under the trees. *DESIGN 8*

MY THOUSAND ISLES VASE

This vase has many paths, so choose a large vase. Now the Thousand Isles, if you have ever been there, has many beautiful homes, islands, Chinese theater and many paths.

On each side in the center of vase I use a Chinese theater scene. Around this I have placed French chateaus and smaller houses. Lovers on benches, climbing the rocky road scene. Now my vase is full, so fire your decals in. I usually end up with about 12 or 14 scenes around my Chinese theater scene.

2. Now you draw many oaks, using capucine brown, dark brown, brown green to make the edge of walkways so it looks like a path to walk on and shrubbery alongside of walkways. Now sponge in with sort of a loose brush the yellow brown (don't let paint run). Put a little capucine brown in yellow brown to darken a little. By this method you will fill in all of the balance of white china. Draw and scroll top of base. Apply Kulp's gold. Fire and polish. *DESIGN 2*

CURRIER AND IVES PLATE IN FRAME

Use 10" or 12" plate. Follow decal center designs now. Use six small oval Currier & Ives around large six inch center Currier & Ives decal. Use five small gold roses, alternating with five small roses a little higher up. Fire.

2. Place circle of gold around center decal. Between one rose and oval decal another circle of gold. Circle each small oval decal with gold line. Use plastic circle and draw five ¼" circles as illustrated. You need your pattern now. Now serpentine and put on your gold band. Fire.

This makes a beautiful plate and you also can put one circle of gold around center decal and filigree around outside of circle and put a larger band of gold on the edge. Fire and polish. *DESIGN 16*

KULP'S ORIGINAL RENDEZVOUS FOR HIS DUCKS

Take a 12" plate. Trim and place ducks or equal birds on your plate separately. Some flying, some maybe looking for food, some drinking water, etc. Divide your plate as you are going to create a little swampy scene. You will also need a little sky for your flying geese. Also put around some of your odds and ends of grass or small flowers or rocks. Fire in all decals.

2. Draw design. Now this is a private meeting place of the ducks or geese, so they will have swamp, rocks, ledges, water, little islands and a few small flowers. Capucine brown and yellow brown are the colors for the ground and rocks. For your water, stripe it a little. Colors aqua and dark green, as where this landing is, you may have a little moss. Make yourself a little tall grass with dark green and olive green. After your design is drawn in and when you are ready, pad in sky, azure blue glaze and elargo rose, like an early morning scene. Take your time and do not try to paint too much in one whole day. Let your paint dry a little and your colors will not run together. Band with gold and fire. Now polish your gold. This will be your masterpiece, for it is truly a study of nature. You will enjoy it and the more you look at it, the more you will find for your ducks to be doing. *DESIGN 14*

KULP'S ORIGINAL DRESSER SET

Place your decals around china, spaced evenly, and fire in decals. Some lines are straight and some curved in this picture and it is a limitation of a spider web. If you will notice you will see a little spider on a straight line. The lines are put in with pen and Kulp's roman gold. Edge with the ball of your finger the fluted top and edge of plates. Use your banding wheel on the circles. Fire .016 and burnish. *DESIGN 7.*

KENNEDY AND LINCOLN PLATES

Place Lincoln picture on 8" plate. Use a border and place it ½" in from edge of plate. Now band on both sides of border a medium line of gold and a gold edge. Now serpentine, after banding plate, the ½" edge you left white. Fire and polish.

Put the Kennedy picture on 8" plate. Put border around border of plate and five gold roses around Kennedy between Kennedy and the border. Fire.

Gold edge and put gold circle on inside of border and fill in solid with gold. Now you have your roses in center and have drawn your partial circles. Place circle around Kennedy and paint in partial circles and serpentine. Fire. Polish gold. *DESIGN 12*

Remember—to use your Kulp's Roman gold—See this chapter on my formula. If you have difficulty please write to me. Enjoy life.

Many years ago, decals were applied to china·by private artists and china manufacturers. But now, time has marched on, we can purchase decals for china firing from commercial companies so that anyone may decorate on china, ceramic or glass.

Also by using a decal as a pattern enables you to have many enjoyable hours of painting. One may study pictures of ages ago and by using the present similar decals can almost match the plate of ages ago. Try a vase now, as well as a plate.

If you have any problems, or you do not understand parts of the book, please write to me.

GEORGE E. KULP,
Lock Box 2103
Ocean View Branch
Miami Beach, Florida 33140

NOTES

MAKE PHOTOGRAPHIC CERAMICS

Reprint Permission granted by C.G.C. & E., Inc.

Would you like to make your own photographic ceramic? You may now do so using a photographic decal prepared from your own favorite photograph. See the attached instruction sheet for details on selecting the decal, selecting the greenware, or china, attaching the decal and firing the decal.

Size of Customer Photograph	Decal Size	Price Per Decal (Cone 018, 010 and 09)
2 ½ x 3 ½"	2 ½ x 3 ½ or *1 ⅞ x 2 ⅝	$1.00
3 ½ x 3 ½"	3 ½ x 3 ½ or *2 ⅝ x 2 ⅝	1.10
3 ½ x 4 ½"	2 ⅝ x 3 ⅜	1.40
4 x 6"	3 ½ x 4 ½	1.80
5 x 7"	3 ¾ x 5 ¼	2.50

*Size Option, 100% or 75% of original photograph. The large size will be made unless the small size is requested. The quality of the photograph may dictate that only the 75% reduced size decal be made. All photographs larger than 3 ½ x 3 ½ are reduced by 75%.

HOW TO MAKE PHOTOGRAPHIC CERAMICS

Send your photograph to C. G. C. & E., Inc., Box 100, Penfield, N.J. He will have a photographic decal fabricated from it. Print you name and address on the back of the photograph for its safe return.

SELECTING A PHOTOGRAPH

The best photographs will have an all white or mostly white background behind the image. Photographs with dark background do not give the high level of appeal as white background photographs. As the photograph becomes larger, insistence upon white background becomes greater. For photograph sizes 4" x 6" and 5" x 7" all white or at least one-half white background behind the subject in the photograph is strongly recommended.

Polaroid photos, portrait type photos and *only colored photographs with very light colored backgrounds* are all possible and will give excellent results.

SELECTING THE TYPE OF DECAL

There are three kinds of decals offered. These are:

1. STANDARD CONE 018 DECAL—for application to any glazed ceramic.
2. SPECIAL CONE 010 DECAL—for application to glazed porcelain.
3. SPECIAL CONE 09 DECAL—for application to cone 06 artware.

Standard cone 018 decals may be applied to any glazed ceramic, including low fired wall tile. When this decal is fired, it has the same appearance and character as commercial overglaze decals. The fired surface is not particularly smooth to the touch.

SELECTING GREENWARE OR A CERAMIC SHAPE

Our photographic decal is easy to apply and fire. A few simple rules are noted here for your benefit in selecting ceramic shapes.

The following ceramic shapes are best to use:

1. All flat areas
2. Straight sided barrels, or curved planes
3. Straight sided cones
4. Very shallow platter

There are many useable shapes possible.

Some shapes should *not* be attempted for the application of the decal. These include:

1. Curved sided barrels
2. Curved sided cones
3. Inside of a deep plate or dish

The decal will not bend to the contour of the three above shapes, and they should be avoided.

APPLYING AND FIRING THE DECAL

1. Soak the decal in cold water (warm water will cause sticking problems).

   Do not permit the two sheets to separate, even though they are free.

   Complete steps 2 and 3 before permitting them to separate.

NOTES

2. Remove decal from cold water. Do not shake off extra water.

3. Place the decal, both sheets still together, against the glazed ceramic area which is to receive the decal transfer. The image is facing you as you want to see it on the ceramic. In doing this, the back up sheet will wet the glaze with just the right amount of moisture.

4. Holding the top sheet in position, slide the bottom sheet out. This permits the thin, image-bearing tissue to contact the glaze.

5. *Run a paint sponge roller (without handle) over the transferred sheet to squeeze out air bubbles, or use a soft sponge to gently brush the bubbles out. Be sure to remove all air bubbles!*

6. Make final positioning of the decal.

7. Again run the roller over the decal, trying not to move it.

8. Allow the decal to dry for 24 hours before firing.

9. Fire the decal to cone 018 to 015. (standard decal).

SPECIAL TECHNIQUES

One interesting capability should be mentioned here. It involves masking the greenware in the area to receive the decal. Underglaze is applied to the ceramic except for the masked area. The mask, which is made of adhensive coated paper, is cut to the exact size of the decal.

Why mask selected areas on greenware before underglazing it?

This is the simplest way for forming a white area surrounded by a colored area. It would not be easier,

for example, to underglaze all of the area and then scrape-off underglaze in a wide area. Even though it may be possible, a clean, fast job with sharp boundary lines would be difficult to achieve.

Why do we want a white area surrounded by a colored area?

A photograph is made up of dark and white areas. The photographic decal is made of black pigment. A photographic decal therefore needs a light cream or white background behind it to set it off.

Many people want photographic ceramics. If the photo is a good one, an excellent ceramic can be made.

The best photographs are black and white, and they have a white background behind a portrait image. Colored photographs are less desirable, but they will work if they have a very light background and the facial tones are relatively light. In all cases, it helps if the clothing is not one solid tone. White is always acceptable for clothing and varying patterns and tones always show-off well. The popular sizes for the photographs are 2½" x 3½" and 1½" x 2¼".

By putting your face on the small china blanks, and firing in your decals, you have an ideal black and white photo. I have used a little yellow brown with a little pink added to it, for the flesh. Colored the hair the desired shade. Colored the dress or outfit. Padded on a background of pastel color. Retraced the facial features with brown or black or color needed. Colored eyes and lips with elargo rose, and put a very, very tiny dot of red in the eye corner at nose (this will bring the face alive). Put in a few shadows where needed. Fire china blanks .018. If your china feels a little rough after firing, simply sand with # 280 sandpaper and if it needs more color, apply colors again and fire. Presto you have a hand painted photo.

MADGE I. SIMMONS

NOTES

DESIGN 1

DESIGN 2

DESIGN 3

DESIGN 5

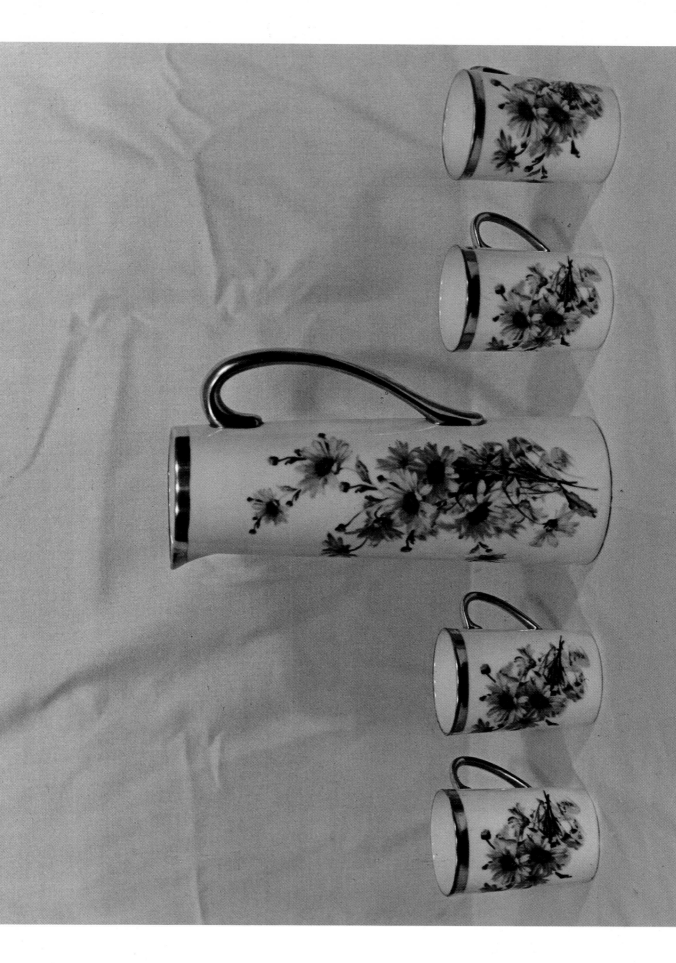

DESIGN 9

DESIGN 11

DESIGN 13

DESIGN 15

ILLUSTRATION 1

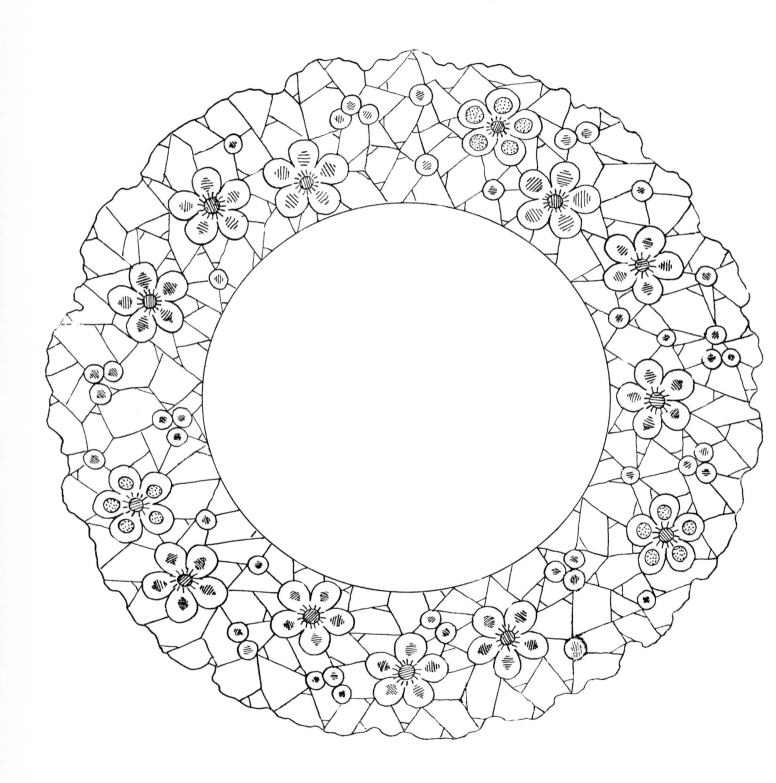

ILLUSTRATION 2

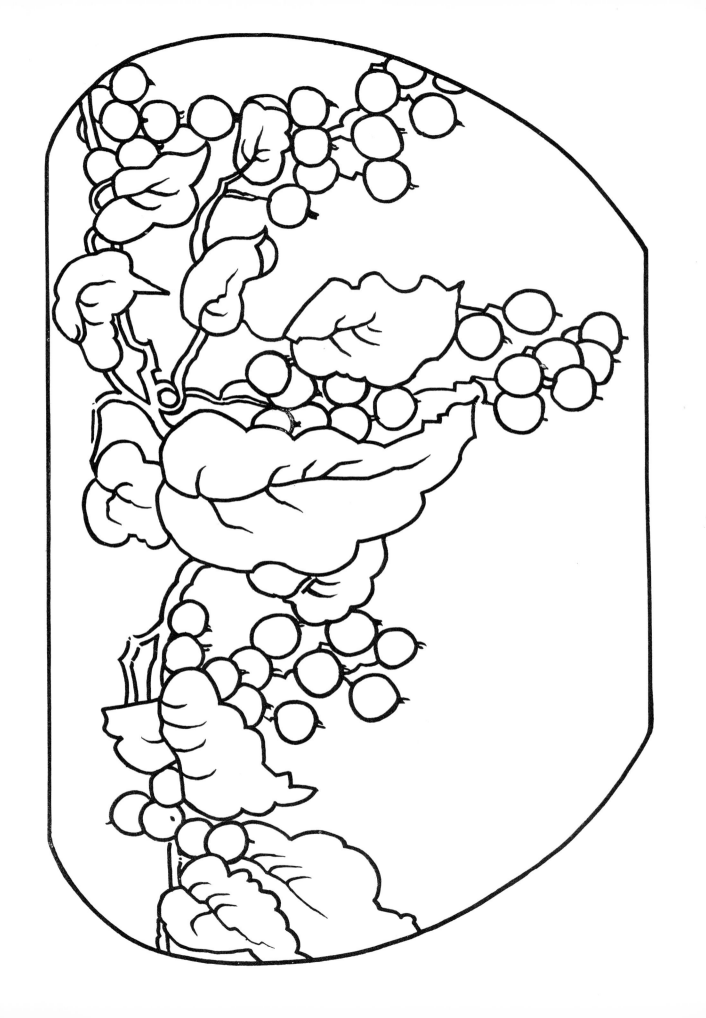

ILLUSTRATION 3

ILLUSTRATION 4

ILLUSTRATION 5

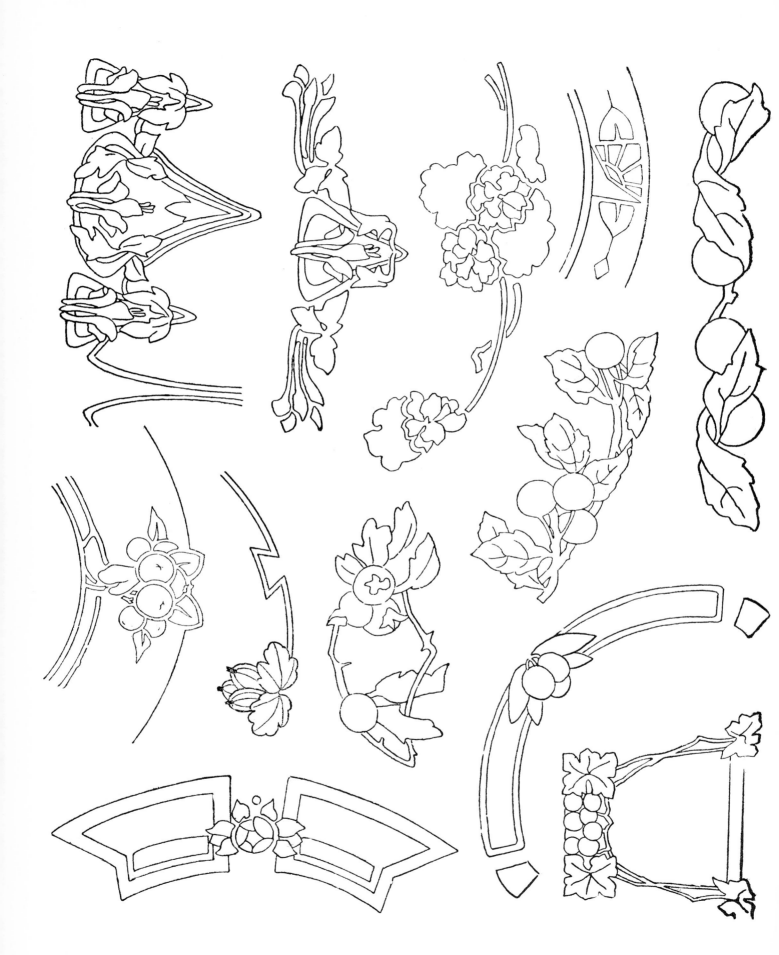

ILLUSTRATION 6

ILLUSTRATION 7

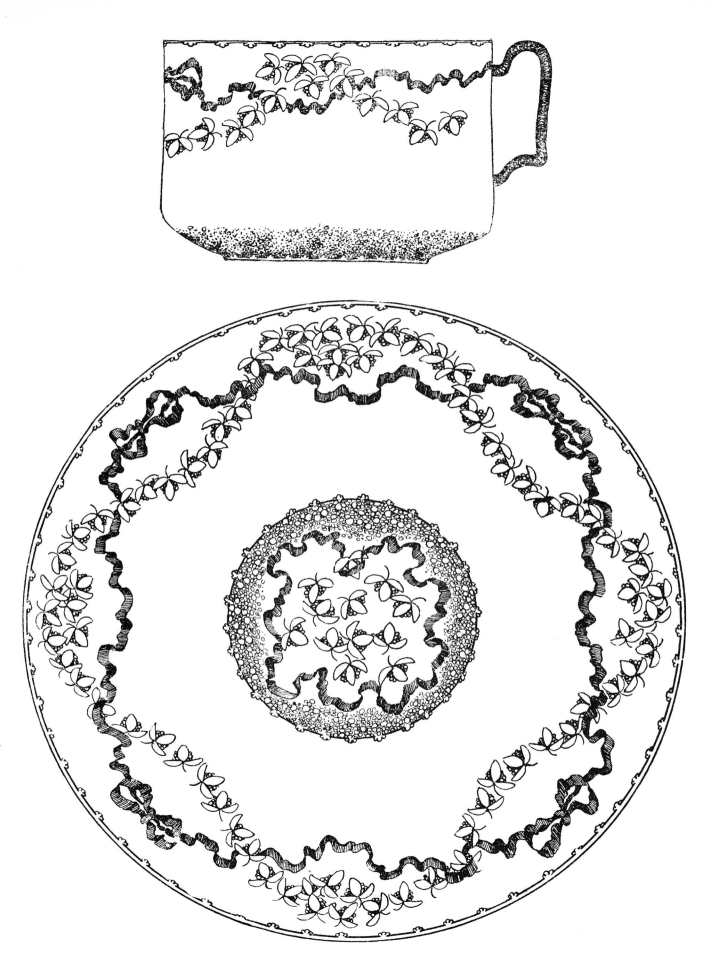

ILLUSTRATION 8

ILLUSTRATION 9

ILLUSTRATION 10

Think big, talk little, love much, laugh easily, work hard, give freely, pay cash, and be kind—it is enough! Do these and you may smoke without danger to your immortal soul.

ILLUSTRATION 11

ILLUSTRATION 12

ILLUSTRATION 13

ILLUSTRATION 14

ILLUSTRATION 15

ILLUSTRATION 16

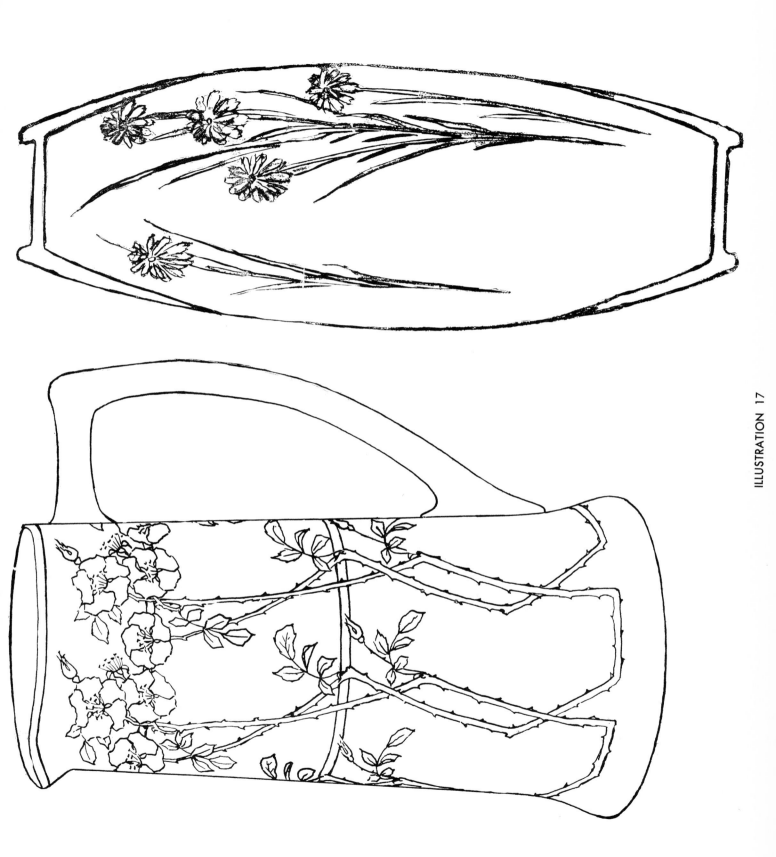

ILLUSTRATION 17

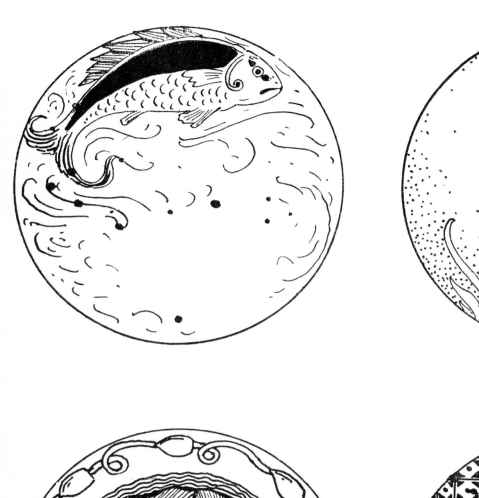

ILLUSTRATION 18

GOLD

ILLUSTRATION 19

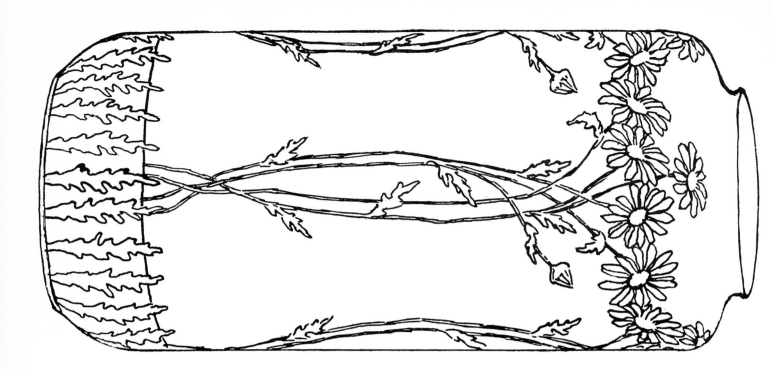

ILLUSTRATION 20

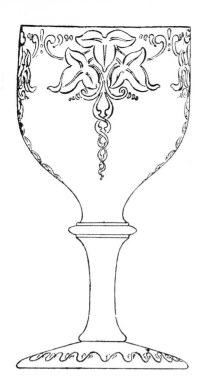

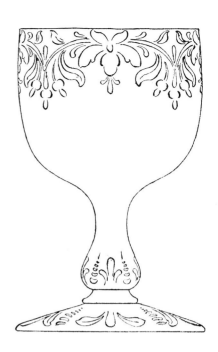

ILLUSTRATION 21

ILLUSTRATION 22

ILLUSTRATION 23

ILLUSTRATION 24

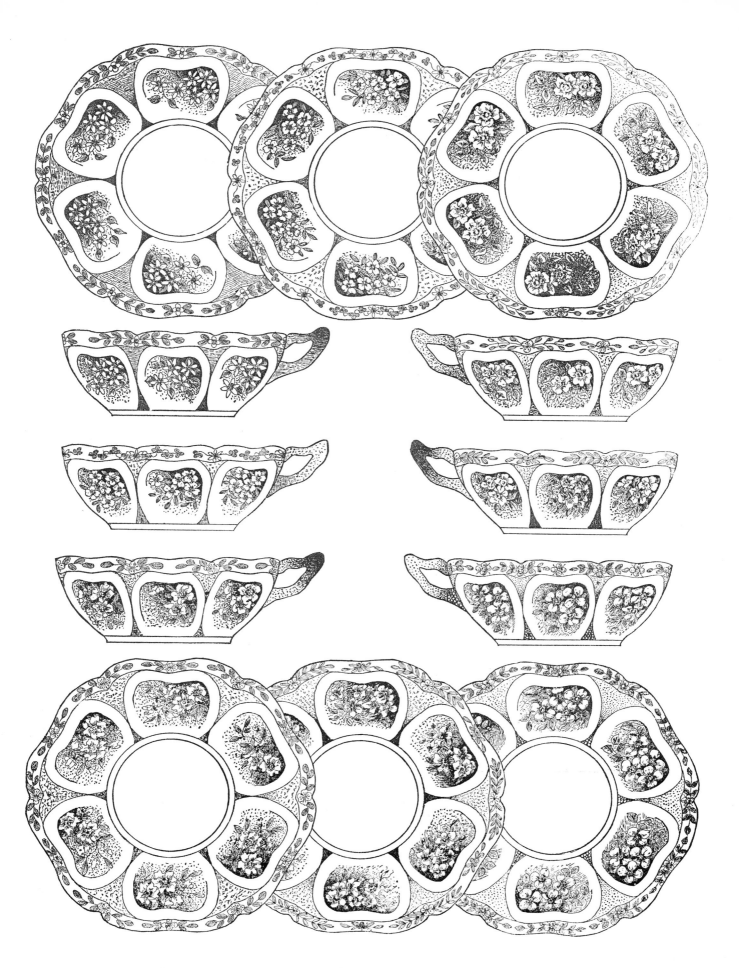

ILLUSTRATION 25

ILLUSTRATION 26

ILLUSTRATION 27

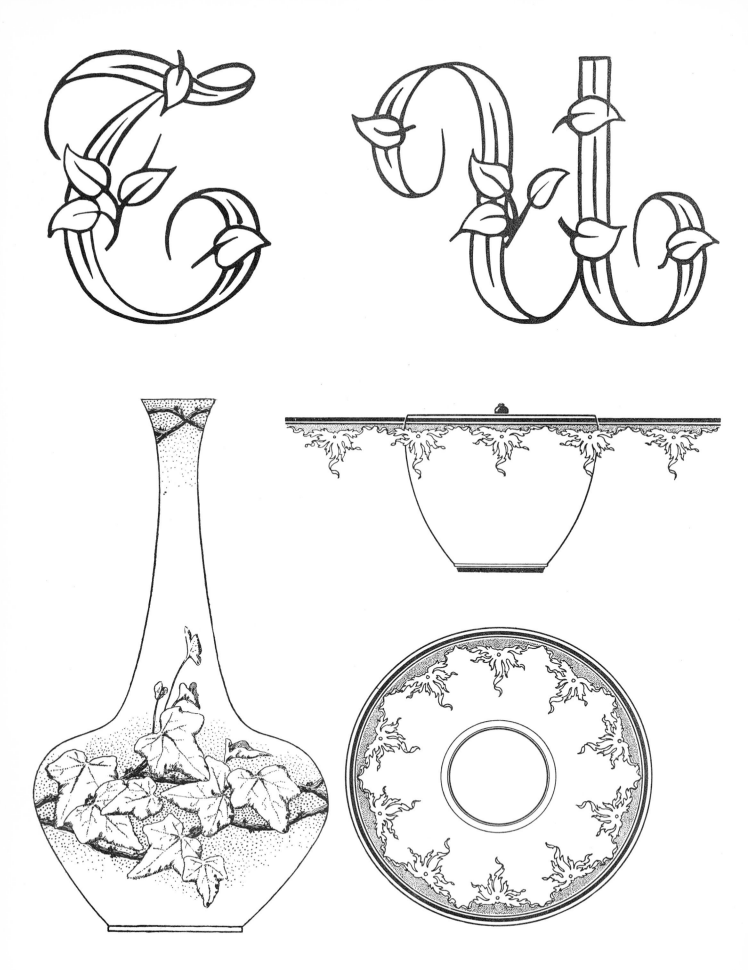

ILLUSTRATION 28

INDEX

INDEX

ILLUSTRATION 32

ILLUSTRATION 31

ILLUSTRATION 30

SELECTED PIECES OF DECORATED CHINA FROM THE ANNUAL EXHIBITION OF THE INDIANA CERAMIC ASSOCIATION 1900

ILLUSTRATION 29